To Seek and To Save
A Memoir and Testimony

Darcy D. Guyant
Commander, U.S. Coast Guard (retired)

First Edition Design Publishing
Sarasota, Florida USA

To Seek and To Save
Copyright ©2022 Darcy D. Guyant

ISBN 978-1506-908-62-5 PBK
ISBN 978-1506-909-72-4 EBK

August 2022

Published and Distributed by
First Edition Design Publishing, Inc.
P.O. Box 17646, Sarasota, FL 34276-3217
www.firsteditiondesignpublishing.com

ALL RIGHTS RESERVED. No part of this book publication may be reproduced, stored in a retrieval system, or transmitted in any form or by any means — electronic, mechanical, photocopy, recording, or any other — except brief quotation in reviews, without the prior permission of the author or publisher.

Scripture marked NIV is taken from the Holy Bible, New International Version®, NIV® Copyright ©1973, 1978, 1984, 2011 by Biblica, Inc.® Used by permission. All rights reserved worldwide.

Scripture marked MSG is taken from The Message, MSG, Copyright © 1993, 2002, 2018 by Eugene H. Peterson

Scripture marked NCV is taken from the Holy Bible, New Century Version®, NCV. Copyright © 2005 by Thomas Nelson, Inc.

Scripture marked GNT is taken from the Holy Bible, Good News Translation®, GNT, (Today's English Version, Second Edition) © 1992 American Bible Society. All rights reserved.

Quotes and excerpts have been used with permission.

To In Sun, my wife, on whom, according to Korea folklore, God bound a golden thread around our big toes at birth, predestining us to this journey through life together. That golden thread, by God's grace, has remained unbroken for over six decades and, Lord willing, will remain for many more decades to come.

To Jennifer and Gordon, who have brought great joy to my life and made me proud to be their dad.

To Gwenyth, who brings more love, joy and zest for life than I can express, and who has made the name "Hal-bae" (Grandpa) my most cherished title.

Preface

A local high school invited me to be their guest speaker for a 2019 Veterans Day school assembly. I happily accepted the invitation. The school's Veterans Day theme that year was "A Legacy of Service." I shared a story from my family's history of military service. My great (x5) grandfather, Luke Guyant, had immigrated to the Colonies from England in the 1760s. He then fought in the Revolutionary War against the British Empire. The only information I have about Luke Guyant is from a written application for veteran's benefits dated 1834 in which he states he was 84 years old. The document gives a brief description of his military service during the war, the units to which he was assigned, battles in which he fought, and injuries sustained in battle.

I would have loved to learn more about his service in the war and his life in general. A journal detailing the experiences of his life, copies of letters written to and from his loved ones, a memoir, or an autobiography would have been very helpful in answering the dozens of questions that come to my mind. What was his life like during this pivotal period of our history? What and who was important to him? Why did he come to the Colonies? Why did he join the rebellion against British rule? It probably never occurred to Luke Guyant that 250 years in the future there would be people interested in knowing more about him and hearing stories from his life.

Since retiring from the U.S. Coast Guard in 2005, I've often thought about writing down some of my experiences and life lessons learned along the way. However, when I thought about the time and effort required to write (ugh!) and how few people would

Darcy D. Guyant

be interested, I would dismiss it as a foolish idea. After all, in the grand scheme of world events and history, I'm insignificant to all but a few family members and friends. It seemed a bit arrogant to think anyone, except for a handful of people, would care at all about my unique experiences, significant events, weighty choices, and life lessons learned.

But then, in 2020, a little girl, my granddaughter, entered this world. I began to think *maybe* someday she might want to know more about her grandpa. What did grandpa do with his life, what was important to him, what influenced his worldview, what guided his choices, and what events molded him into the person he was? Lord willing, she may get answers to many of the questions from me firsthand. But there is no guarantee I'll be around long enough to share all that is on my heart, or she simply may not really care or be interested until she is much older. And what about her children and her grandchildren? Maybe someday they might want to know more about their ancestors, just like I've wondered about mine from 250 years ago.

Ultimately, however, and much more significant is the fact that my story isn't just about me. The Lord Jesus Christ has guided my life often in ways unseen and unknown to me at the time. God has allowed hardships, pain, and heartaches, but always as opportunities to learn, trust, and grow to become more like Christ. But God has also bestowed uncountable blessings and has no doubt preserved my life on numerous occasions. Why? Only God knows for sure, but I suppose it's because my mission on this earth is not done yet. When my mission is complete and in His perfect time, He will bring me home. I look forward to hearing, "Well done, my good and faithful servant."

Until then, I've still got work to do and a few stories to tell.

What is your life story without Christ?
It is one with no main character and without a plot.
It is a brief, meaningless mix of droning words until an anticlimactic and sudden end.
It is little more than a display, faux book-prop at IKEA.

—John Bartlett

CHAPTER 1

A Beer Commercial

> *For I know the plans I have for you," declares the Lord, "plans to prosper you and not to harm you, plans to give you hope and a future.*
> —Jeremiah 29:11, NIV

January 26th, 1980

Alone at the Controls

The throttle was pushed full forward to maximum power and the engine revved loudly. The rapidly spinning propeller blade directly in front of me was just a blur. I glanced down at the flight instruments and saw the aircraft was about 300 feet above the ground and we were climbing. The pointer on the airspeed indicator was holding steady at 70 knots. I looked over at the pilot seat next to me. It was empty!

My adrenalin surged as the full realization of my situation became clear. I was sitting at the cockpit of an airplane, flight controls in my hands, several hundred feet in the air, and I was alone. I had mixed emotions about the other seat being empty, but I could not afford to dwell on that. I needed to focus. I was solely responsible for control of this airplane. People's lives were literally in my hands. I took a quick look below me. I saw several roads and a highway packed with many cars, a cramped neighborhood, an elementary school to my right front, a full Walmart parking lot to my left, and Lake Erie directly in front of me, stretching to the horizon.

I couldn't help but think, "If those people down there knew what was happening in this plane flying over their heads at that very moment, they would probably be concerned, very concerned."

So, how did I end up in this situation?

September 17th, 1979, Lincoln Park, MI

It's Miller Time

It was the beginning of my senior year of high school, and I was starting to feel the clock ticking down. I still had 9 months of school left, so I wasn't overly concerned. Yet. But I knew I needed to start thinking seriously about what I was going to do after high school. At that point, I really had no plan. I did not have an interest in—or even feel drawn toward—any particular type of job or career field. I did like being outside, fishing, camping, and such. So, maybe something like a game warden or park ranger? I had just spent the summer working on my grandpa's farm and enjoyed that. So maybe something involving farming or agriculture? I had no specific plan or direction, and I was starting to feel some pressure.

I was downstairs in the TV room, watching Monday Night Football with my dad and brother. A commercial came on during a break in the action and it immediately caught my attention...as any good commercial does. It started out with the camera panning across a beautiful lake. The surface of the deep blue lake was as smooth as glass, not a hint of wind disturbed the water. The lake was surrounded by tall evergreen trees. Far beyond the trees were rugged snowcapped mountains. The only sound was that of a Loon calling its mate. It was a beautiful, serene setting.

A moment later, an airplane, with floats instead of wheels, appeared as it banked left just over the treetops. The plane swooped in low over the treetops and descended to a smooth landing on this glassy surface of the lake. The plane coasted across the water and then up to a beach. Several guys climbed out of the plane and start fishing. They had a grand time hauling in huge trout.

The screen then faded to a scene with the guys sitting around a campfire, cooking their catch over an open fire. Their tents and the airplane were poised in the background and firelight flickers off the trees. The guys laughed, swapped stories, and drank beer. Then a message appeared in the center of the screen and a familiar jingle began to play. The message read, "It's Miller Time!" and the jingle goes, "When it's time to relax, one beer stands clear....". It's a beer commercial!

I sat watching, riveted. As the commercial ended, I had a sudden revelation. "That's it!" I suddenly knew what I wanted to do for a living. I wanted to be a bush pilot! I'd fly float planes into remote wilderness lakes, taking people fishing, hunting, and camping in the wilderness. I already had experience camping and fishing. All I needed to do was learn to fly an airplane. I turned to my dad and asked, "How does someone get trained to fly airplanes and become a pilot?" He said he didn't know exactly, but maybe I could just go to the airport and pay someone to teach me to fly.

I grabbed the phonebook and turned to the Yellow Pages. Sure enough, there was a listing for a business at the Grosse Isle Airport that rented airplanes and provided flight instruction. Grosse Isle Airport was located on a large island in the south end of the Detroit River, right where the river emptied into Lake Erie. It was only about 20 minutes' drive from where I lived in Lincoln Park, Michigan.

The Next Saturday

I borrowed Dad's car and drove down to the airport. I found Grosse Isle Flight Services and parked next to their building, which appeared to be an airplane hangar. To me, the airport seemed very large, with two long runways and several hangars scattered around the perimeter of the airfield.

It was quiet, except for the sounds of some chirping birds and that of an airplane flying somewhere off in the distance. Parked on the tarmac near the building was a small high wing airplane, which I would later learn was a single engine Cessna 152. A silver fuel truck was also parked nearby with markings on the tank that read, "100 LL." A man and woman were walking around the plane looking it over, apparently getting ready to take it up on a flight.

On the back side of the hanger was a glass door with a sign above it that read "Office." I walked in, and the first thing I noticed was a couple of guys in the corner looking at a large colorful map hanging on the wall, which I would later learn was a VFR Sectional map. Behind a glass display counter to the left was a guy seated at a desk. He looked up and asked how he could help. I told him I was interested in getting some information about flying lessons. He came over to the counter, handed me a brochure, and then spent several minutes explaining how their Cessna flight training program worked, what it would cost, the number of flight hours required, and so on. I could feel my excitement growing. He told me for $10 he could take me up for a 30-minute introductory fight. I asked him to schedule me for 1 PM the next afternoon, since I still needed to get permission from my parents.

The money I had earned working on my grandpa's farm over the summer was enough to make the initial payment for the flight training program and still pay for a few hours of flight instruction. I also had an after-school job where I would earn just enough each week to pay for 2 hours of flight instruction each weekend. My parents gave me permission to give it a try. They may have had doubts I'd stick with it, but it was my money and my time, so it would be my loss if I quit.

The Next Day

The next afternoon, I drove back down to the airport. The same gentleman I had talked to the previous day took me up on the 30-minute orientation flight. I didn't get airsick or have any "fear of heights" apprehension, so I enrolled in their training program. The Cessna Flight Training Program enrollment fee included a book, a map (VFR Sectional), an E6B (also known as a Wiz Wheel, which is sort of a slide rule, but round), a logbook, and a very cool red flight jacket with a Cessna patch on the front. I wore that flight jacket everywhere: school, work, church, and of course, when I flew. I scheduled my first official lesson for the next Saturday.

October 7th, 1979, Grosse Ile Airport, MI

Raising Doubts

The next Saturday, I meet Ken, my flight instructor. Ken had been a U.S. Marine Corp fighter pilot. He flew F-4 Phantom fighter jets for 5 years, including several combat missions in Vietnam. He was a serious, no nonsense, tell it straight, very intense kind of guy. He spoke like a Marine, using "colorful" language occasionally, and he had high performance expectations. I was definitely intimidated by him, but he knew his stuff, and I figured who better to teach me how to fly than a former jet fighter pilot with combat experience. I did wonder why a F-4 fighter jock was working as an instructor pilot and flying Cessna 152s, but I was afraid to ask.

I continued taking lessons on the weekend, usually one hour on Saturday and another hour on Sunday. I was enjoying the flying part of the training, but the studying for the written tests was difficult. Turned out there was a lot more to being a pilot than just flying the airplane. I had to learn about meteorology, navigation, airplane mechanical operations, flight instruments, the physics of flight, mastering the use of the E6B Whiz Wheel, FAA flight rules, and more. I was beginning to have doubts about pursuing a flying as a career.

First Solo!

On January 26th, 1980, I was again practicing takeoffs and landing with Ken. After about 30 minutes, Ken told me to taxi over to the side of the runway so he could get out. It was time for my first solo flight! I was nervous, but also confident in my fledgling skills. Ken gave me a few last minutes instructions as he was unstrapping:

- Do 3 takeoffs and landings, then come back to pick him up.

- Use the aircraft tail number ID when making radio calls, like usual, but add "solo" to the call. This would warn other planes in the area to watch out and cut me some slack.

- And lastly, he said, "Don't mess up, kid," though his language was more colorful than that.

He closed the door, and then did something I'd *never* seen Ken do before. He smiled. That was all the confidence boost I needed.

I taxied back to the runway center line, made a radio call, applied full power, and used my rudder pedals to stay on the center line as the plane accelerated to takeoff speed. At takeoff speed, I pulled back on the yoke, adjusted my pitch up attitude to maintain the climb airspeed and adjusted the rudder pedals to keep the slip ball centered. At about 300 feet in the air, I looked over at the left pilot seat just to confirm. It was in fact empty! I was really flying solo! It was exhilarating. I'm sure I was grinning ear to ear. I was hooked. I knew for sure what career I'd pursue after high school. I was going to be a pilot.

High School to Flight School

Toward the end of my senior year, I joined the Army to enter their "High School to Flight School" program. The Army would train me to fly helicopters, which wasn't really what I wanted to do, but the flight training was "free" and I was getting paid to do it.

I did look into Air Force and Navy flight training, but the Army was the only service that would take me right out of high school. The other services required a bachelor's degree first or attendance at a 4-year academy, and even then, there would be no guarantee of flight training. The Army offered the quickest route to becoming a pilot, even if it meant flying helicopters. I saw this as a steppingstone to someday flying "real" aircraft.

During my 7 years in the Army, I attended night school and earned a bachelor's degree from Embry-Riddle Aeronautical University. After earning a degree, I thought about leaving the Army and joining the Air Force to become a jet pilot. The hit movie *Top Gun* had just come out in the theaters, so I was also thinking about the Navy. But, after more consideration, the thought of being on a ship, separated from my family, and trying to land on a pitching and rolling ship at night and in the middle of the ocean sounded absolutely crazy.

I took the Air Force entrance exams, but at the time, the Air Force had an overabundance of pilots and wasn't accepting new applications to flight school.

In their hearts humans plan their course, but the Lord establishes their steps.
—Proverbs 16:9, NIV

Army to Coast Guard

God closed that door to the Air Force, but He opened another one, a door to an opportunity I had never previously considered. That new door was the U.S. Coast Guard.

One evening, I was talking with a friend after a class we were both taking. Stewart told me he was planning to transfer to the

Coast Guard when he finished his bachelor's degree. This piqued my interest, so I also started looking into this as a possible option. (Sad note: Stewart Dietrich perished in a helicopter crash on April 26th, 2022.)

Shortly after having the seed of an idea planted by Stewart, I spotted an advertisement in the *Army Times*. The *Army Times* was a weekly newspaper with a target readership of active-duty Army personnel. The advertisement solicited applicants for the Coast Guard's Direct Commission Aviator program. Army warrant officers, which I was at the time, would receive a commission as an ensign. It was a direct commission, so there was no need to attend Officer Candidate School.

The more I researched the Coast Guard the more I liked the idea of using my helicopter piloting skills and my flight experience to perform search and rescue missions and actually help people. I left the Army in October 1987, was commissioned as an ensign, and become a Coast Guard helicopter pilot, but that's another story...actually, many stories.

Bucket List Item

I never did become an Alaskan bush pilot, but that beer commercial did spark an interest in flying, which led to a long flying career, which also included a couple of years flying helicopters (helos) in Alaska.

I never flew airplanes again after earning my private pilot license in high school, nor did I get the opportunity to land on water in a float plane. However, in a strange twist of fate, I have landed helicopters on the water, but that, again, is also another story.

My "Bucket List" still includes flying in a float plane to a wilderness lake in order to camp, fish, sit around a campfire with friends, swap stories, and of course, have a beer. Lord willing, I'll cross that off my list one of these days.

Giving Credit Where Credit Is Due

The phrase, "God works in mysterious ways," is a well-known cliché. While there is no verse in the Bible that uses these exact words, the sentiment is true. God's ways are mysterious to us simply because we are not omniscient, omnipotent, or omnipresent like God is.

I believe God used a simple beer commercial to plant a seed and spark an interest. The origin of my 25-year career as an officer in the Army and Coast Guard and as a helicopter pilot can be traced back to that TV commercial. I had never considered flying as a career possibility until that very moment. I am also grateful to my parents for consenting to and supporting my pursuit of this sudden, off the wall interest sparked by a beer ad.

Unbeknownst to me at the time, God was guiding my steps, even though I didn't really know Him yet. Often, God used people to plant seeds, provide council, and offer encouragement to proceed in a particular direction. He also used circumstances to open some doors and close others. Paths of various possibilities were available, and choices had to be made. Sometimes I made bad choices or chose my own path, but God was still there.

For my thoughts are not your thoughts, neither are your ways my ways,' declares the Lord. 'As the heavens are higher than the earth, so are my ways higher than your ways and my thoughts than your thoughts.
—Isaiah 55:8-9, NIV

Chapter 2

Red Baron 19

Yet you do not know what tomorrow will bring. What is your life? For you are a mist that appears for a little time and then vanishes.
—James 4:14, NIV

April 1st, 1982, near Wonju, South Korea

The Ride of The Valkyrie

With my adrenaline pumping, I zipped along at 90 knots (100 mph) just above treetop level, staying low and hugging the contours of the terrain. I was flying the 2nd aircraft in a formation of five Army UH-1H "Huey" helicopters. The lead aircraft was to my left front, at about my 10 o'clock position. We were in a tactical "free cruise" formation, meaning I needed to keep that aircraft in sight at all times, but I was free to maneuver anywhere from its right rear to left rear position. There were 3 more aircraft in the formation behind me, somewhere close.

The terrain on my right rose steeply with terraced rice paddies climbing up the mountain side. An occasional pagoda, small red tiled roofed houses, and "happy mounds" (grave sites) zipped by outside my door. My head was on a swivel, scanning from left to right, keeping track of the lead aircraft, watching the undulating terrain, and keeping an eye out for potential hazards in front of us. I didn't bother looking inside at the instrument panel. My job was to stay focused outside. It was the responsibility of the other pilot, Jerry, seated in the left seat, to monitor the instruments, navigate, and make radio calls. However, at the moment, we were operating in radio silence.

We were about 10 minutes from our landing zone where we were to pick up a platoon of Korean special forces soldiers and then fly them to a location behind enemy lines. Our crew chief and gunner were seated in the open back doors with M60 machine guns mounted and ready. I heard "The Ride of The Valkyrie" playing in my head as our formation made its way up the valley. *(In the movie* Apocalypse Now, *there was a scene where a formation of Army helicopters comes flying in low over the water blaring "The Ride of The Valkyrie" over loud speakers. As a senior in high school, I went to see that movie and left the theater more motivated and determined than ever to become an Army helicopter pilot.)*

I had graduated from flight training just 4 months earlier at Fort Rucker, Alabama, on December 1st, 1981. I was 19 years old, the youngest pilot in the unit, maybe even the youngest ever assigned to the 201st Aviation Company (Air Assault), also known as the "Red Barons." There was nowhere else I'd rather be! I felt on top of the world and was thinking I'm already a pretty hotshot pilot. After all, they don't just let anybody become a Red Baron. Right? I was sitting pretty high on my horse. However, I was about to get bucked off that high horse and be given a dose of the real world.

Mission Briefing and Launch

Just prior to taking off, I attended the mission briefing with the other 9 pilots. The unit I was assigned to, The Red Barons, was deployed to a field location about 50 miles south of the North Korean border. Deploying to the "field" was sort of like going camping, living in leaky tents, sleeping on cots, field toilets, no showers, frequently eating food from cans (C-rations), and so forth. In other words: not a lot of fun.

We had been in the field about 1 week already, flying missions in support of Team Spirit 82. Team Spirit was a large military preparedness exercise conducted annually in South Korea. On that particular morning, our mission was to fly five aircraft to a landing zone (LZ) about 20 minutes away, pick up a platoon of Republic of Korea (ROK) special force soldiers and insert them at a location behind simulated enemy lines. I had initially been assigned to fly as copilot in the lead aircraft, but just prior to the mission briefing, the commanding officer (CO) decided he wanted someone with more experience in the lead aircraft. Apparently, there were going to be some high-level Korean generals observing the mission at the pickup zone.

I was swapped into the copilot seat of the 2nd aircraft of the five-ship formation. Our CO, a major, would be flying the trail (5th) aircraft. During the Vietnam War, our CO had been shot down and sustained severe burns to his head, arms, and hands. The major was a hard charging, rough talking, battle scared (literally) Vietnam veteran. I, on the other hand, was a 19-year-old kid fresh out of flight school. The major had a reputation for being very demanding and unforgiving of mistakes. I found him to be very intimidating. During that morning's mission, his unit was being observed by high level "brass." I was perfectly fine with not being in the lead aircraft on this mission...in case things went wrong. And oh boy, did they!

As the 2nd aircraft in the formation, we had to be ready to take over as Lead in case something happened to the 1st aircraft. Jerry, the pilot in command of our helo, wanted me on the controls flying while he navigated. This was well before the days of GPS, so we'd be navigating the "old fashion way" with a 1:50,000 contour map. Knowing exactly where we were and staying on the planned route was not easy, especially at low level altitude moving along at 90 knots. I loved navigating, and I was pretty good at it, but for that mission, I was very happy to have the controls in my hands and the map in Jerry's hands.

Low and Fast

All five aircraft took off simultaneously in a tight staggered right formation and climbed to about 500 feet. At a prebriefed point on the route to the landing zone, Lead descended to terrain flight altitude. I followed him down to about 50' above tree level and loosened up the formation to what was called a Tactical Free Cruise. In a Tactical Free Cruise formation, all aircraft stayed close enough to the aircraft to their front so that the door guns can provide suppressive fire if needed, but we also had the freedom to maneuver left or right of the aircraft to our front. This allowed each aircraft some freedom to maneuver and take advantage of the terrain to remain low and seek concealment from potential enemy ground fire. My adrenalin was pumping. I was jinking up, down, left and right, just above the rice paddies and treetops. I was keeping an eye on the lead aircraft but also scanning ahead of us, looking for potential hazards.

We were now about 10 minutes out from our LZ. I had Lead in sight about 200 feet away, just ahead, and to my left at about my 10 o'clock position. He was just a little lower than I, flying up the center of the narrow valley. I was slightly higher due to the rising terrain on my right. Directly ahead, I spotted the top of a power line pole sticking up just above the tops of the trees. I increased power slightly to cross the power lines right at the power pole. I said to Jerry, "I've got the wires in sight; I'm crossing at the pole."

Jerry's head was down, looking at the map, so he didn't see the power pole or the wires. At that instant, I realized the power lines from that pole stretch down and across the valley! I looked over at Lead and key the microphone to radio a warning of the wires directly ahead. It was too late.

Wires!

At that instant everything seemed to go into slow motion, like I was watching a scene in a movie. I saw Lead fly directly into the wires, not thin telephone wires, but high-tension power cables. The helo caught one wire right across the front windscreen. Sparks began to fly. Another wire pasted just over the top of the cockpit and snagged the vertical mast of the rotor system. The force of the impact on these two wires caused the nose of the aircraft to pitch upward, toward the sky. One of the rotor blades hit the wires and disintegrates into 100s of pieces as it sliced through them. Sparks continued to fly. I watched as the remaining stub of the one rotor blade continued to rotate while the other blade remained intact. The nose of Lead was now pointing nearly vertical. In real time, this all happened in about five seconds, but the weird slow-motion effect made it seem much longer. To this day, I still have those 5 seconds of "slow motion video" burned into my memory.

I key the radio and yell, "Wires! They hit the wires!"

Jerry, with his head down, hadn't seen Lead hit the wires. He heard me yell on the radio and thought I had said, "We hit the wires!" His eyes snapped up from the map and saw we were about to cross over a power pole, just like I said we were doing a moment ago. He keyed the intercom and asked, rather franticly, "What wires?!"

I yelled, "Lead! Lead hit the wires!"

Jerry looked over to our 10 o'clock position, where Lead should have been. They were gone.

After crossing the power pole, I made a left turn to go back to where I'd last seen Lead, its nose pointed straight up in the air, rotors still turning, but with half of one blade gone. As I came around, I saw the other 3 aircraft turning and climbing to avoid wires and flying debris. I spotted black smoke rising from a stand of trees on the edge of several rice patties. This was obviously where the helo had gone down. I flew to the location and started a left-hand orbit over the crash site, about 200 feet above the trees. Jerry was on the radio talking to the other 3 aircraft, reporting what we could see. The downed helo was laying on its left side, already burning. It was surround by a thick stand of trees, branches obscuring the area around the burning aircraft. We could see no sign of the 4 crewmembers who were in the helo. All any of us could see was thick black smoke billowing up through the trees.

The remainder of that morning is a bit of a blur in my memory. One aircraft immediately climbed to altitude to report the crash and call for a medical evacuation helo in case there were survivors. The other two helos landed in a rice patty near the crash site. Jerry and I were directed by the CO to return to our base camp and pickup personnel to help with securing the crash site.

As horrific as this crash was, all 4 crewmembers unbelievably survived. The worst injuries were to the pilots, Mike and Jeff. When the 1st wire hit their windscreen, it shattered into many tiny fragments. The force of the impact caused the visors on their helmets to snap up into their helmets, exposing their eyes to the glass. Both had minor eye injuries, and all had bruises, but there were no broken bones, serious lacerations, or burns.

The force of the impact had pitched the helicopter nose to nearly vertical, which dissipated their forward momentum. The helo then fell straight down, with tree branches and the aircraft tail, somewhat cushioning their fall. It was a miracle nobody was impaled by a tree trunk or branch as they crashed to the ground. A tree did puncture the fuel tanks, which caused the aircraft to catch fire shortly after it came to rest. All 4 crewmembers were conscious, able to unstrap their seat harnesses and climb out before the helo became fully engulfed in flames.

There, but for the Grace of God, Go I

This accident was a pivotal moment in my maturing as a person and as a pilot. It could have been me flying that aircraft, hitting the wires, crashing, and burning. I was originally supposed to be me flying lead, but I was swapped out at the last minute.

This crash sobered me to fact that what I was doing was not some risk-free adventure. There were real life and death consequences at stake. Exercising poor judgement, not comprehending the risks, or not taking the risks seriously could get me or others seriously hurt or killed.

I admit, this accident shook me up and gave me a jolt of reality. This incident was a key moment in my maturing as an aviator. If not for this wakeup call, I could have been a "gung-ho invincible cowboy," taking unnecessary risks and making poor judgements.

Except for the loss of one Huey, it was a cheap lesson that would pay huge dividends in the years that followed.

Red Baron 19

On June 1, 1982, 3 months after the crash and 6 months after graduating flight school, the commanding officer signed off on my qualification as a UH-1H "Pilot in Command." I would now have my own Red Baron callsign. I was given the callsign "Red Baron 19." It seemed an appropriate designation since I was still 19 years old—for one more day anyway.

A couple months later, I would be designed as a unit trainer (UT). As a UT, my responsibilities would include training newly assigned pilots on the designated routes and procedures for operating around the Prohibited Flight Area surrounding the city of Seoul, known as "P73." The South Koreans were serious about violations of P73. They would shoot down violators of this airspace.

I also trained unit pilots on routes and procedures for flying near the Demilitarized Zone (DMZ) between North and South Korea. Again, flying into or across the DMZ will get you shot down, held prisoner by North Korea if you survive the crash, and possibly spark an international incident. It has happened before. I did *not* want any of that to happen, so I took this responsibility very seriously.

Red Baron 19 would continue to darken the skies of South Korea for 18 more months. I had the opportunity to fly many incredible missions all over the country, from landing near "the fence" at the edge of the Demilitarized Zone (DMZ) with North Korea, to an island off the southern tip of the Korean Peninsula, to remote landing pads on some of the country's highest mountains, to planning, briefing, and leading multi aircraft low level tactical missions.

But I also had some the of closest calls of my flying career in Korea. I experienced my own extremely close call with a set of wires at night in a fog shrouded valley. I also had an extremely close near midair collision, avoided only by something (or someone) prompting me to look straight up and spotting another helo ten feet directly above us who hadn't seen us either. Both incidents could have ended very badly, but God had other plans.

Mrs. Red Baron

The most important life changing event happed about 1 year into my tour in South Korea, and it had nothing to do with flying. By God's good grace, I met a beautiful young lady shortly after Christmas in 1982. In Sun and I starting dating, and on July 21st, 1983, we were married.

Now, more than 39 years later as of this writing, with two awesome children and one equally awesome grandchild, we both thank God for His tremendous blessings in our lives and in our marriage.

Every good and perfect gift is from above, coming down from the Father of the heavenly lights, who does not change like shifting shadows.
—James 1:17, NIV

Helicopter Pilots Are Different

The thing is, helicopters are different from planes. An airplane by its nature wants to fly, and if not interfered with too strongly by unusual events or by a deliberately incompetent pilot, it will fly. A helicopter does not want to fly. It is maintained in the air by a variety of forces and controls working in opposition to each other, and if there is any disturbance in this delicate balance the helicopter stops flying; immediately and disastrously. There is no such thing as a gliding helicopter.

This is why being a helicopter pilot is so different from being an airplane pilot, and why in generality, airplane pilots are open, clear-eyed, buoyant extroverts and helicopter pilots are brooding introspective anticipators of trouble. They know if something bad has not happened it is about to.

Harry Reasoner,
Approach Magazine, Nov 1973

Chapter 3

Rescued!

> *God rescued us from dead-end alleys and dark dungeons. He's set us up in the kingdom of the Son he loves so much, the Son who got us out of the pit we were in, got rid of the sins we were doomed to keep repeating.*
> —Colossians 1:13-14, MSG

My U.S. Coast Guard career commenced in October 1987 at the Coast Guard Training Center in Yorktown, VA. At TraCen Yorktown, I attended the 2 weeklong Direct Commission Aviator (DCA) orientation course. Immediately following the DCA course in Yorktown, I reported to the USCG Aviation Training Center in Mobile, AL. My next phase of training was learning to fly the HH-52 Sea Guard helicopter and to perform Search and Rescue operations.

Darcy D. Guyant

November 19th, 1987, Mobile Bay, AL

Water Landing

Water splashed on the plexiglass chin bubble down near my feet, which were resting on the helicopter's tail rotor control pedals. The helicopter bobbed up and down slightly while rocking back and forth in the choppy wind-driven waves. We were floating on the water!

For the 7 years I had been flying Army helicopters, it had been drummed into my head that flying over water was dangerous—never do it! Most Army pilots were not trained, nor were Army aircraft equipped, to operate over water. So, it was a little unnerving to see and hear waves lapping against the side of the helo just outside my open cockpit window.

Transitioning from the Army to the Coast Guard was a fairly significate culture shock. The Coast Guard had very different missions, aircraft, customs, terminology, rank structures, equipment, and operating environments. Getting comfortable with operating over the water, which was nearly all of the time, required a definite change of my mindset.

I was at the Coast Guard's Aviation Training Center (ATC) in Mobile, AL, learning to fly the HH-52 Sea Guard helicopter. The HH-52 had a unique capability over most other helicopters. It was designed to land on the water and, most importantly, take off again from the water. The bottom of the HH-52's fuselage was shaped like the hull of a boat, and it had sponsons (out riggers) on each side to help stabilize the aircraft while sitting on the water. I had loved flying the Army's UH-1 "Huey" for the past seven years. The Huey was sleeker, faster, and more powerful. The Huey *could* land on the water. But only once. It would roll over and sink—very quickly. So, in that respect, the HH-52 had a definite advantage over my beloved Huey.

On this particular day, my instructor, Gabe, and I were over Mobile Bay practicing approaches, landings, and takeoffs from the water. I had already performed a couple of water landings when we received a radio call from the Coast Guard Group Mobile operations center. They had received a report, via phone, from a concerned citizen on shore of an overturned boat in Mobile Bay, not far from where we were operating. Group Mobile asked if we could divert and assist.

My First Search and Rescue Mission

Gabe responded to the call and advised operations that we were diverting from training and heading to the reported location. I was excited and eager. I was now on my first ever search and rescue mission! Within a few minutes, we were over the reported location and immediately spotted the white hull of a small, overturned boat. We could see one person clinging to the partially submerged hull, and he did not appear to be wearing a life jacket. The man clinging to the hull was not moving, not waving for help, or even looking up at us. His arms were stretched out over his head gripping the keel of the boat, apparently holding on for dear life. We had no idea how long he'd been in the water, but judging by his behavior and lack of movement, we suspected he was exhausted and possibly succumbing to hypothermia. The USCG Group Mobile OpCen advised us that a boat had been dispatched, but it would be 20 minutes before it would arrive on scene. Gabe decided we should not wait; that man needed help now!

Attempting to hoist the victim from a hover using the hoist cable and rescue baskets was quickly ruled out. Gabe was concerned the helicopter's rotor wash would blow the man off the hull. The man still hadn't moved or looked up at us, so Gabe doubted he even had the strength to climb into a rescue basket. We did not have a rescue swimmer on board with us during this flight, only a flight mechanic/hoist operator.

Gabe decided the best course of action was to land on the water, taxi in close, and do a platform pickup. The HH-52 had a metal platform that could be attached outside the cabin door. The platform would hang suspended just above water level. This platform would allow the flight mechanic, back in the cabin of the aircraft, to step out of the helicopter, grab the survivor, haul him up out of the water onto the platform, then pull him inside the aircraft.

The cabin door and rescue platform were on the right side of the helo. I was seated in the right pilot seat, so I would be on the controls, "taxiing" the helo on the surface of the water toward the victim. The plan was to land the helo on the water with the man just outside the helicopter's rotor wash. We did not want the wind from our rotor blades to accidently blow him off his tenuous perch. Once landed, I was to "water taxi" the helo to position, placing the cabin door and rescue platform close enough for the flight mech to step out and pull the man onto the platform and then into the helo. I had done one practice pickup early in the afternoon, but not with a person, just with a ring buoy used for training.

Platform Pickup

Gabe made the approach. He landed the helo on the water with the man at our 2 o'clock position, relative to the nose, and just outside the disturbed water caused by the rotor wash. Gabe instructed me to take the flight controls and the flight mech began giving me "conning commands" (movement directions) to maneuver the helo to where he wanted it. Water occasionally splashed on chin bubble window from the choppy waves as was we bobbed, rocked, and slowly edged our way closer to the overturned boat. I was able to keep the survivor in view until he disappeared from my sight behind the right sponson. I called out, "Lost target," and the flight mech kept up his conning commands.

He talked me into position saying, "Easy forward and right 15; easy forward and right 10; hold forward, easy right; hold, I'm stepping on the platform." The hull of the overturned boat bumped lightly against the extended platform. The flight mech stepped out and dragged the victim onto the platform. Once there, the flight mech assisted him with climbing into the cabin.

With the survivor now on board the helo, Gabe took the flight controls back and picked us up to a hover. The mech closed the door as we transitioned to forward flight for the short hop to the airport a couple miles away. A waiting ambulance would take the man to the hospital. As we flew toward the airport, I looked back at the survivor to see how he was doing. He was sitting on the cabin floor, the flight mech's jacket draped over his shoulders. He was hunched over, soaking wet, shivering, obviously exhausted, but alive. I turned the cabin heat controls to maximum.

So, less than 2 months into my Coast Guard career, still in training, and I had just participated in my first rescue. Helping people who were in distress was the reason I decided to leave the Army and join the Coast Guard. When I looked back into the cabin and saw our survivor sitting there, I knew beyond a shadow of a doubt I had made the right career choice. My transition from Army to Coast Guard aviator was well underway.

HH-52 Sea Guard

I flew the HH-52 for eight months, logging a little over 200 hours flight time. It's fuselage height, stubby nose, and sponsons sticking out on each side created a lot of wind drag (resistance). The 52 was not fast, and at times, I felt like I was piloting a barn door. But, in the hands of highly skilled, experienced, and brave aircrews, this aircraft saved many lives during its 25-year history of service. I was privileged to have had the opportunity to fly such a unique and storied aircraft before they became museum pieces or scrap metal.

All HH-52 aircraft in the Coast Guard inventory were eventually replaced with the brand-new HH-65A Dolphin. The HH-65A was sleek, fast, had two engines and a bunch of other modern features that made it a dream to fly. But, just like a Huey, it could land on the water...but only once.

The Museum of Flight in Seattle, WA, has an HH-52 on display. Its tail number is 1415. This aircraft was based at Coast Guard Air Station Port Angeles, WA. My first Coast Guard duty assignment was at Air Station Port Angeles, so I flew #1415 on many occasions. On July 31, 1988, I had the privilege of flying this aircraft for 2.1 hours on the final search and rescue mission of its 25 years of service. The very next day, August 1st, Air Station Port Angeles began operating the HH-65A full time. Coast Guard #1415 was flown one final time to Boeing Field in Seattle, where it would eventually go on display in the Museum of Flight.

July 15th, 2007, Petersburg, KY

Rescued!

It has been nearly 20 years since I participated in my first helicopter rescue that windy day on Mobile Bay and I am now retired from the Coast Guard. My wife and I moved to Kentucky so I could work for a parachurch organization. It was my first day at my new job. My new supervisor, Kirk, met me in the lobby and led me through a labyrinth of doors and hallways to his office. As I followed Kirk into a large, shared office space containing numerous desks, I spotted a painting hanging on the wall behind a desk. The painting instantly grabbed my attention, something about it looked very familiar, like I had seen it before.

It took a few moments, but then it came to me. I had seen the man in the painting before, or rather someone who looked very similar. The man in the painting was nearly identical to the man I had seen clinging to his overturned boat in Mobile Bay nearly 20 years before!

The guy in the painting was wet and clearly exhausted, his face showing a look of deep anguish. He was not wearing a life jacket, only a thin shirt. The water around the man was wind swept, looking as if the rotor wash of a helicopter hovering nearby was creating waves on the surface of the water. The image of the man in the painting was strikingly similar to what I remembered of the man clinging to the overturned boat in Mobile Bay twenty years earlier.

Rather than clinging to an overturned boat, however, the man in the painting clung to a large piece of wood. The piece of wood may have been a piece of his ship, which may have broken up in a storm, or had been smashed on a reef, or maybe even destroyed in a naval battle at sea. I stepped closer to see the title of the painting, which read, "Rescued!" The signature of the artist, in the bottom right corner read, "Darrin Hoover."

When I realized the piece of wood the man was clinging to was in the shape of a cross, the deep meaning and symbolism of the painting dawned on me. The man was clinging to a cross! His source of hope and salvation, even in the midst of a raging storm, was a cross. Even while enduring pain, isolation, and severe trials, he found hope of rescue in that cross, the only thing keeping him afloat. But, of course, the deeper meaning of the painting is in who that cross represents and the hope of rescue found in Him.

Christ Jesus had endured trials, pain, suffering, isolation, anguish and death on a cross. He did this willingly and as an act of love in order to bear the burden of our biggest problem, which is our sin. It is sin that separates us from God the Father, but Jesus bridged the gap which separates us from God. That bridge is represented by a cross, an old rugged cross, where Jesus took the penalty for our sins upon Himself.

> *For God was pleased to have all his fullness dwell in him, and through him to reconcile to himself all things, whether things on earth or things in heaven, by making peace through his blood, shed on the cross. Once you were alienated from God and were enemies in your minds because of your evil behavior. But now he has reconciled you by Christ's physical body through death to present you holy in his sight, without blemish and free from accusation.*
> —Colossians 1:19-22, NIV

Just like the man in the painting, we too may feel adrift in this life, unable or unsure of how to save ourselves, exhausted from the effort of trying to feel worthy, defeated by failures, with no hope of rescue in sight. But God saw my plight, and not just mine, but all of us. God says to anyone who will listen, "I have a way of rescue for you! Grab ahold and put your faith and trust in My Son, Jesus! Cling to this old rugged cross and what it represents, which is the sacrifice Jesus, My Son, made for you on this cross, and you will be saved!"

Nearly 18 years prior to seeing this painting, I had been rescued. After ignoring or pushing away the lifeline extended to me for the first 26 years of my life, I finally recognized my need, reached out, and grabbed ahold. I share the details of exactly when and how my "rescue" came about later.

This painting, *Rescued,* now hangs on a wall in my home. After learning the significance of this image to me, Kirk arranged for me to have it as a gift. The painting had been bought at a garage sale for just a few bucks. The canvas has a few scratches, and the frame is a little beat up, but regardless, it is one of my most valued possessions. Every time I see it, I am reminded of my Rescuer.

Due to copyright laws, I am unable to show a copy of *Rescued* in this book. I encourage you view this painting online by searching, "Rescued by Darrin Hoover," on the internet or visiting this web address:
www.christcenteredmall.com/stores/art/hoover/rescued.htm

The Old Rugged Cross

George Bennard wrote a hymn which superbly expresses the significance of the cross. The lyrics convey the deep meaning and representation of the cross much better than I could do in my own words.

On a hill far away stood an old rugged cross,
the emblem of suffering and shame;
and I love that old cross where the dearest and best
for a world of lost sinners was slain.
Refrain:
So I'll cherish the old rugged cross,
till my trophies at last I lay down;
I will cling to the old rugged cross,
and exchange it some day for a crown.
O that old rugged cross, so despised by the world,
has a wondrous attraction for me;
for the dear Lamb of God left his glory above
to bear it to dark Calvary.
In that old rugged cross, stained with blood so divine,
a wondrous beauty I see,
for 'twas on that old cross Jesus suffered and died,
to pardon and sanctify me.

To that old rugged cross, I will ever be true,
its shame and reproach gladly bear;
then he'll call me some day to my home far away,
where his glory forever I'll share.

HH-52 full autorotation landing to the water. Photo taken by and used with permission of CAPT Bill Peterson (USCG ret), author of *A Miracle at Attu: The Rescue of CG-1600*.

Chapter 4

Tropical Storm Beryl

A helicopter in the hangar is safe, but that's not what helicopters are built for. A pilot on the ground is safe, but that's not what pilots are trained for.

August 15th, 1994, coast of the Florida Panhandle, Gulf of Mexico

Into the Maelstrom

A wall of dark clouds extended into the sky as high as I could see. Flashes of jagged lightening arc through the clouds from one end to the other. The sheets of heavy rain look like a dark blue, almost black, impenetrable wall. Even at this distance, I could see the clouds churning, the violent winds and turbulence rolling them over and over. Tropical Storm Beryl was building toward hurricane strength in the Gulf of Mexico, and it was rapidly pushing its way northward toward the Florida coastline.

I had a front row seat to the unfolding drama to the east. In stark contrast to what my eyes could see in the distance, I was surrounded by blue skies, marred only by a light wind that barely rippled the surface of the turquoise water of the Gulf of Mexico. I looked up and down the white sand beaches of the Florida panhandle and saw throngs of vacationers lounging on the beach, no doubt with cool beverages in hand, and building sandcastles. Many were enjoying the balmy Gulf of Mexico water, swimming, riding jet skis, sailing, and fishing. I was sure many were also keeping an eye on the eastern storm in the distance, warily eyeing the potential threat to their vacation fun. Some may even have been marveling at the distant display of nature's awesome power, just as I was.

However, all those people on the beach enjoying their vacation were oblivious to the peril of three men caught in the middle of that storm, struggling to stay alive and keep their disabled fishing boat afloat. Those three men held on for dear life as they were mercilessly tossed by 20-foot waves and battered by 60-mile per hour winds. They knew they were in serious trouble, and if help didn't arrive soon, they would probably die. Unlike the 1,000s of people below, I and the others in the helo with me, were very aware of their peril.

My "front row seat" was in the cockpit of a Coast Guard HH-65A helicopter, and we were flying directly toward the unnerving menace growing in size and strength to our east.

"May Day"

An hour earlier, I had been at my desk preparing for an afternoon training flight. I was an instructor pilot at the U.S. Coast Guard's Aviation Training Center in Mobile, Alabama, where my primary job was to train Coast Guard pilots to fly the HH-65 helicopter. On occasion, we would be tasked with flying urgent search and rescue missions, much like we had been asked to do on that day.

Our Operations Center had received a call from the Rescue Coordination Center in New Orleans asking if we had a helo available to respond to a "May Day" call from a fishing vessel with 3 people on board. The disabled fishing vessel was about 100 miles to our southeast, caught in the middle of Tropical Storm Beryl. It was slowly taking on water and sinking. Air Station New Orleans did not have a helo available to respond at the time. Jeff, a fellow HH-65 instructor pilot, and I were already scheduled for a training flight together, so we quickly shifted into search and rescue mode.

We received the distressed boat's position and did some quick mission planning. We determined we had fuel enough to make it to the location of the sinking boat, conduct 3 hoists to get the men off the vessel, and still land at a small airport in Apalachicola, Florida. However, we knew fuel was going to be tight, so everything needed to happen like clockwork.

A Coast Guard HU-25 Falcon jet took off shortly after we did. The Falcon could fly 3 times faster than our helicopter, so they went ahead to locate the fishing vessel and provide us with an updated position. We did not have enough fuel to spend time searching for the boat, so knowing the exact position of the vessel was critical. We had to get straight to work, hoisting the crew up if we were going to have any hope of rescuing them and reaching the airport before we ran out of fuel. The Falcon jet would stay with us for the entire mission, orbiting overhead to act as a communications relay and keep an eye on us in case something went wrong. It was always nice to know we had a cover aircraft overhead watching out for us.

We passed by the vacationers on the white beaches of the Florida coast at about 500 feet. We zipped along at about 120 kts., which is the speed that gave us the maximum range we could fly with the current amount of fuel on board. Our weather radar showed a thick dark green band of very heavy rain directly in our flight path. I had been marveling at the awesome sight of the storm from a distance, but as we got closer, I began to feel a touch of anxiety as the reality of punching headlong into that heavy curtain of rain grew closer by the minute. As we prepared to penetrate the storm's outer band, I said a quick prayer, made sure my seat harnesses were cinched tight, lowered our altitude to 300 feet in order stay visual with the surface, and slowed down to a speed better suited for turbulence. It was about to get very bumpy! The guys on the fishing boat just needed to hold on for another 20 minutes.

The HU-25 Falcon crew arrived on scene well before us and radioed an updated position, which we plugged into our GPS. Even knowing exactly where the boat was located, it was still very difficult to spot. The heavy rain dropped our visibility to about half a mile. The boat was painted white, so it blended into the 15-to-20-foot breaking waves and white frothy wind streaks on the surface of the water. However, we spotted the boat fairly quickly thanks to the Falcon crew's position updates. I put us in a right-hand orbit over the vessel so the flight mechanic/hoist operator (FM) and rescue swimmer (RS) could see the boat and evaluate the situation.

On Scene

None of us liked what we saw. The 40-foot fishing boat was broadside to the 60 mph winds and the breaking waves. It rolled about 20 degrees to port then to starboard while riding up and down the huge waves. Hoisting the men directly from the boat was out of the question due to antennas and other rigging whipping wildly back and forth. Waves were occasionally breaking over the boat's deck, so it was probably not going to stay afloat much longer. With input from the FM and the RS, we quickly came up with a plan. The boat's radio was no longer working so we couldn't relay our plan to crew. The RS would have to go down and talk to them in person.

We turned to make our approach directly into the intense wind and descended to a hover, placing the boat on our right front. We had 20 minutes of fuel remaining before we needed to depart for the closest airport. The FM hooked the RS to the hoist cable and prepared to lower him into the water, placing him just downwind from boat. We hovered in closer to minimize the amount of swimming the RS had to do to reach the boat. The men on the boat had inflated a small life raft and tied if off to the downwind side. This would be helpful. When the RS reached the water, he released the hoist cable and swam to the edge of the raft, battling the wind and waves the whole way. Holding on to the raft, the RS yelled to the men to, one at a time, get into the raft and then get into the water with the RS. The RS would swim them away from the sinking boat a safe distance and then help them get into a basket being lowered from the helo. He told them he'll do this 3 times.

The hoist of the 1st man went as planned, though he was in severe pain with possible broken ribs. Once inside the door of the helo, the FM tipped the basket on its side and helped the man crawl out. He grimaced and groaned loudly, his severe pain obvious as he crawled out of the basket. We were now down to 10 minutes of on-scene fuel remaining. It was taking way too long.

Just as the FM prepared to send the basket back down for the 2nd crewman, I noticed the fishing boat's stern settling lower into the water. The 2 men still on board felt their boat starting to sink out from under them, so they untied the raft from the boat to prevent it from getting pulled down with the sinking boat. Unfortunately, when they untied the raft, the 60-mph wind caught it and sent it flying away on its own.

Now the men had no choice but to jump into the water and get away from the sinking vessel. Thankfully, they had life jackets on, and the RS was right there to help them get ready for the next basket hoist. The fishing boat took one last wave over the port side then slowly sank out of sight.

We quickly moved in, lowering the basket for the second crewman. With the boat now completely gone from sight, we found ourselves conducting a "no reference" hoist, which depended entirely on voice commands from the FM over the intercom to know where to position the helo. We got into a hover just above the wave tops to minimize the blow back of the hoist cable and basket. Looking at our increasingly critical fuel situation, I suggested trying to get the remaining two men in the basket together in the next hoist, but the FM said, "There's no way; there're too big!"

Bingo!

The second survivor was now in the basket coming up and approaching the cabin door. A warning light flashed on the instrument panel. We were at "0" minutes for our fuel "bingo." "Bingo" meant we had to depart the scene NOW in order to land at our planned destination with a 20-minute fuel reserve. In an HH-65A helo, this was about 200 pounds of fuel. Helicopters measure fuel quantity in pounds, rather than gallons.

The third survivor and the RS were still in the water waiting to be recovered from the water. Leaving them in the water and heading for shore to refuel was *not* an option. It was very unlikely they both could survive in this storm without a raft—the RS maybe, but the fishing vessel crewmember probably not. We did have our own survival raft onboard the helicopter, which we could drop to them, but they would have to inflate it and climb in while getting battered by 60-mph wind and 20-foot seas. We quickly decided to continue with one last hoist attempt and, if the hoist was not working out quickly, push our raft out the door and head to shore to refuel.

We *had* to pick up both the RS and third crewman during the next hoist, and it had to be quick. Back in the cabin, the FM disconnected the basket and attached a "rescue strop" to the hook. The RS would see the rescue strop and understand we needed to pick them up together. The RS would wrap the strop under the arms of the survivor and hook him to the hoist cable, then he would hook himself to the cable with his harness, allowing us to bring them both up at once. The strop was made from a flexible foam material and very light, therefore it would blow back toward the tail rotor of the helo in the 60-mph wind. We needed to attach some extra weight to the hoist hook so that it would go down and not flutter in the wind like a kite. The FM attached as many weight bags as we had on board. I told him to also attach the aircraft's cabin fire extinguisher.

As Jeff hovered in for the final pickup, I got on the radio and explained our dilemma to the Falcon crew still orbiting overhead. They gave us a heading to fly to the closest point of land, just in case we didn't have enough fuel to make it to the airport and needed to make an emergency landing somewhere.

The hoist cable went down, and the RS was able to grab the rescue strop, disconnect the weight bags, and fire extinguisher, and let them sink. He wrapped the strop around the survivor, hooked his harness to the cable, and gave the FM a thumbs up. In less than 30 seconds, they were ready for pickup.

We got the RS and third survivor inside the door and immediately began to transition to forward flight. Our flight computer was now indicating we would land with 10-minutes of fuel remaining, which is about 100 pounds of fuel. I have landed with slightly less than 200 pounds of fuel on a couple of occasions, but never 100 pounds! This made us all very concerned.

Now with a 60-mph tailwind giving us a push, we screamed toward shore at almost 200 mph over the water. The visibility was about half a mile, and we could not climb above 300 feet due to the cloud ceiling above us. The HU-25 Falcon crew had called ahead and arranged for an ambulance to meet us at the airport to transport our 3 survivors to the hospital—assuming we made it to the airport. That prospect was still very iffy.

Jeff and I discussed transferring the remaining fuel into one tank to keep at least one engine running, but then decided against it. If we did have to land on the beach or somewhere short of the airport, it would be better to have two engines, rather than just one engine or, God forbid, no engines.

Calculated Risks

We finally spotted some land dead ahead. The Falcon crew advised us this was St. George Island, and the airport was still about 5 more miles due north. We'd be flying over a stretch of water again before reaching the airport. It was time to make a quick go / no go decision. Landing on the beach or other unimproved area in a storm of this magnitude was not without its own set of risks. We also had a survivor onboard with unknown, possibly severe injuries who needed to get to a hospital ASAP.

We were still zipping along at close to 200 mph over the water. We had no warning lights indicating fuel starvation was eminent and we'd be over the airport in another 2 minutes. We made a decision to "go" for the airport.

It was a long 2 minutes, but then we spotted land again, and then the runway. We decelerated, turned into the wind, dropped the landing gear down and landed on the tarmac near where the ambulance was already waiting. We landed with 100 pounds of fuel remaining, just as predicted. To non-pilots, 100 pounds might sound like a lot of fuel and 10 minutes sounds like plenty of time, but it is not. It would be like having the low fuel light in your car come on and then deciding to continue to a gas station still 50 miles away while in Death Valley and with 120-degree temperature outside, no phone, and no water to drink. But if you run out of gas in your car, you pull over and coast to a stop, but in a helicopter, you, well, you fall out the sky—very rapidly.

After a couple of hours on the ground, the storm subsided enough to safely refuel the helo. We rechecked the weather and decided we could safely return home to Mobile. The weather improved quickly and dramatically the further west we flew. It wasn't long before we saw crowds of people on the beach again, still enjoying the surf and sun, oblivious to what we and the 3 survivors had just endured.

Awards

Our entire aircrew was awarded the Coast Guard Commendation Medal for saving the lives of those 3 fishermen. I confess, I was initially disappointed with the level of that award. This may sound petty and ungrateful, but I felt that mission met the criteria for the awarding of an Air Medal, if not for the entire crew, at least for the rescue swimmer. But the powers that be apparently did not agree.

I stewed about this for a while, but then remembered why I joined the Coast Guard. It wasn't about medals, recognition, or personal glory. It was about saving lives and making a positive difference in this world.

Three men went home to their loved ones that night. I never met the guys we saved that day or learned anything about them, not even their names. I hope they went on to live happy productive lives, have children and grandchildren, and positively influenced our world and the lives of others. I will never know this side of heaven.

God used me to *seek* out and to *save* those who were most certainly going to be lost in that storm. I did my part in fulfilling God's sovereign plan to give those gentlemen more time on this earth. I'm satisfied with that.

The Lord Is My Pilot

The Lord is my Pilot, I shall not stray off course or glide path.
He lighteth my way across dark waters;
He steereth me through the stormy nights;
He keepeth my Flight Log;
He guideth me by His Star of Holiness for His Name's sake.
Yea, though I fly midst the thunders, lightning, and turbulence of Urgent SAR,
I shall fear no danger, for Thou, O God, art with me.
Thou preparest a safe landing before me in your Homeland Security of Eternity.
Tho anointest the waves with oil, and my hoist and rescue swimmer save those in distress.
Surely, sunlight and starlight shall favor me all the missions I fly.
And I will dwell securely in the hangar of my Lord forever. AMEN.

Adapted from the 23rd Psalm by Victor Primeaux, CDR, USCG (retired).

Chapter 5

The Bar Hopper

The Ones You Remember

In the movie *The Guardian* there is a scene where the young, inexperienced rescue swimmer, played by Ashton Kutcher, asked the old, grizzled rescue swimmer legend, played by Kevin Costner, about the number of people he had saved during the course of his career. Costner reluctantly replied, "Twenty-two."

Kutcher, surprised by a number much lower than expected, given Costner's reputation and years of experience, said to him, "Oh. That's great, it's not 200, but still, 22 lives saved is great."

Costner corrected him, "No, 22 is the number of lives I could not save. Those are the only ones I counted." Those were the lives he remembered, the lives he was unable to save, the ones who stuck with him and maybe even haunt his memories.

The following story is one such number for me.

Saturday morning, April 29th, 1989

Gone Fishing!

John and his long-time fishing buddy, Peter, finished loading their gear into John's truck. John's 18-foot Lund fishing boat was strapped down tight and ready for the 3.5 hours trip to Clallam Bay, WA, for 2 days of salmon fishing. John said goodbye to Sarah, his wife, and reminded her of their plan to be home by 8:00 p.m. Sunday night. John and Peter, both in their 50s, have been taking trips to the northwest corner of Washington to fish together for the last 8 years. They make this trip to Clallam Bay at least once a year to fish. Both men have experience fishing in the Strait of Juan de Fuca, which is the large body of water that separates the United States and Canada and connects the Pacific Ocean with Puget Sound. They are equipped with a radio, emergency signal flares, and life jackets. The boat and motor have been well maintained. The name of their boat, *Bar Hopper*, is painted on the stern.

11:00 p.m., Sunday, April 30, 1989

Overdue

Sarah, John's wife, began to worry. It was 11 p.m. and John had not yet returned home, nor had he called to let Sarah know they were on their way. Peter's wife had not heard from them either. Both were growing concerned. Their husbands were experience fishermen and had trailered their boat out to that location many times over the years, normally returning home by early evening. They lived near Tacoma, WA, so the drive was about 3.5 hours from where they normally launched their boat in Clallam Bay. It was very unusual that they had not returned home by that time or called to let them know they would be late. Both men were also scheduled to be at work the next day.

Sarah initially called the Clallam County Sheriff Department, but they transferred her to the Coast Guard Operations Center in Port

Angeles, WA. She reported her husband and his friend as being overdue from a fishing trip near Clallam Bay, WA. Clallam Bay was within the Group/Air Station Port Angeles area of responsibility. The group duty officer (GDO) took down all the information Sarah could provide about her husband's fishing plans, the boat, equipment on board, their experience, and so on.

After gathering all the relevant information, the GDO called Coast Guard Station Neah Bay. Station Neah Bay is a boat station located on the most northwest tip of Washington and the closest USCG unit to Clallam Bay. The GDO directed them to have someone drive to the boat ramp to check for the truck and trailer. About 30 minutes later, Station Neah Bay personnel called back to confirm their fears. The fishermen's truck and empty trailer were still parked at the boat ramp in Clallam Bay.

Station Neah Bay was directed to get a boat underway to begin searching for the overdue men. The helicopter from Port Angeles also launched to begin a night search, hoping to spot a flare or some other type of signal from the overdue men. Coast Group Port Angels began making "urgent marine information broadcasts," asking vessels in the area be on the alert for the missing vessel. The helicopter crew flew a sortie, searching the shoreline of the Strait of Juan de Fuca out past Neah Bay and down the coast. The helicopter landed at the Station Neah Bay helo pad to refuel before continuing to search the Strait of Juan de Fuca north of Clallam Bay, working northward toward Canadian waters. The Neah Bay boat crew also continue to search throughout the night. The helicopter returned to Port Angeles after its second sortie. That crew had been up all night, so it was time to send out a fresh helo crew to conduct a first light search.

7:00 a.m., Monday, May 1st, 1989

Good News!

At around 7:00 a.m., USCG Station Neah Bay sent one of its personnel over to the boat ramp in Clallam Bay to confirm that the truck and trailer were still there. About 30 minutes later, Station

Neah Bay called the Port Angeles Operations Center and reported that the truck and trailer were gone; they were no longer parked at the boat ramp. Apparently, the fishermen had come back sometime during the night, loaded their boat, and departed, presumably for home. The helicopter and boats stood down from the search and returned to their bases.

The wives of both men were called and advised that the truck and trailer were no longer parked in Clallam Bay, so it was assumed they were on their way home. The wives were greatly relieved by this news. The wives were asked to have the men call the Coast Guard Operations Center when they returned home. We needed to get some information from them for our Search & Rescue reports before the case could officially be closed.

12:00 p.m., Monday, May 1st, 1989

Assuming the Watch

I entered the Operations Center of Coast Guard Group/Air Station Port Angeles a few minutes before noon. I was one of the two pilots assuming Search & Rescue (SAR) duty for the next 24 hours. The off going duty pilots were in the OpCen preparing to give us a change of watch briefing.

Our briefing commenced precisely at noon and consisted of a summary of SAR operations performed during the previous 24-hour period, including any cases still in progress. The only case still open was that of the fishing boat, *Bar Hopper*, and the 2 men reported as overdue from fishing near Clallam Bay. They had reportedly come back in sometime during the night. Their truck and trailer were gone from the boat ramp during a check earlier in the morning. We were briefed to expect a phone call from one of the men at some point to officially close out the SAR case.

Renewed Concern

With the change of watch briefing completed, I took over manning the Operations Center desk. About 30 minutes later, I received a call from Sarah, John's wife, telling me their husbands *still* had not returned home and she was very concerned again. Sarah told me this was completely out of character for John and Peter not to call and update them on their location and on any delays. They were both very conscientious men. During our conversation, Sarah mentioned their daughter was getting married in two weeks and she *really* needed her husband to get home okay.

Sarah suggested that perhaps they had had an accident while driving home the previous night. Her voice was shaky, and I could sense the deep concern and rising panic in her voice. I assured her I would make calls to the local sheriff and police departments to check for any accidents reported between Neah Bay and Tacoma involving a truck and trailer. After talking with Sarah, I started to get a feeling that something definitely was not right.

On a hunch, but truly hoping I was wrong, I called Station Neah Bay and told them to send someone over to the Clallam Bay boat launch again, just to doublecheck and confirm the truck and trailer were still gone. I made sure they had the correct truck description and license plate numbers. It would take them about 30 minutes to drive over there to take a look. The office for the other pilot on duty with me was next to the OpCen. He was the senior duty officer, so I told him about the call from one of the wives and that I had Station Neah Bay doublechecking the boat launch. He agreed with checking with local law enforcement for any reported accidents. I called the county sheriff's department. They had no reports of trucks involved in any mishaps in the last 72 hours.

Hopes Dashed

About 30 minutes later, the Operations Center's phone rang. I saw from the caller ID that it was USCG Station Neah Bay calling me back. The commanding officer of the station was on the phone. He quickly said, "The truck and empty trailer *are* still at the boat ramp. The person who checked for the truck earlier this morning did not check *both* parking areas and missed it." The truck and trailer *had* been parked there the whole time!

The men's wives had gotten their hopes up based on wrong information. Now their worst fears were about to be confirmed. Their husbands were missing...were still missing! I felt sick. We had wasted the entire morning assuming the men were okay, and no one had been searching for them.

I hung up the phone and dashed to the operations officer's office (OPS). The senior duty officer was already there. I told them that the CO of Station Neah Bay had confirmed the truck and trailer were still at the boat ramp. OPS uttered a couple of expletives and quickly headed to the Operations Center, telling the SDO and myself to get airborne ASAP. He would pass a search plan to us over the radio once we were in the air. I reminded OPS that the wives were not yet aware of this news and were still expecting their husbands to be arriving home. He hung his head and quietly said, "I'll call them."

I could only image the reaction of the wives and other family members with this awful news. My heart went out to them. I grabbed my flight gear and quickly headed to the aircraft determined to find those two men and fully confident they would be found and saved.

Massive Search Effort

At this point, the Coast Guard's District Command Center in Seattle took over the planning and coordination of the search operations. It would become the largest search operation in which I was ever involved. Multiple U.S. Coast Guard aircraft and boats as well the Canadian Coast Guard resources saturated the Pacific Northwest Washington coasts and waterways. The search lasted 3 days with 1000s of square miles searched and 100s of resource hours expended. I flew 5 search sorties over the next 3 days. Everyone involved in the search was determined to find the two missing men. By the 3rd day of the search, determination became desperation as we began to realize time was about to expire.

Search Suspended

After 3 days of intensive searching, we'd found not a single trace of the boat, the men, or any of their equipment. The search was suspended. Nothing was ever found. No debris, no distress calls, no oil slicks, no bodies, and no clues. There was lots of speculation about what might have happened, but never any evidence. It was as if the boat and the men had vanished. I suspect whatever did happen to the men on the *Bar Hopper* must have been very sudden and catastrophic. It's very likely the outcome of our search would have been the same, even if the error causing the delay had not occurred.

I don't know exactly how many people I rescued or assisted during my career as a Coast Guard pilot. There are several successful missions that stand out in my memories, but the missions I remember most vividly, the ones that cause me to wonder what more could have been done, are those who could not be reached in time or were not found at all.

The mystery of the *Bar Hopper* is one that has stuck with me. I have often thought about and wondered what happened to those guys, but I will never know this side of heaven. One day, when I do get to heaven, I'll have lots of questions. One will be, "What happen to the men on the *Bar Hopper*? Why couldn't we find them?" Hopefully, I'll even get a chance to meet them in person.

Chapter 6

Green Gold Wings

Electrum is a naturally occurring alloy of silver and gold. The man-made alloy of silver and gold is chemically similar to electrum but is usually called "Green Gold."

October 15th, 1987 – Coast Guard Training Center Yorktown, Yorktown, VA

First Day as an Ensign

    I stood in front of a mirror wearing my U.S. Coast Guard uniform for the first time. It looked and felt very foreign on me. Someone at Coast Guard Headquarters had waived their magic pen and "poof," a new Coast Guard officer appeared. The stroke of a pen transformed an Army chief warrant officer into a brand spanking new, direct commission aviator (DCA), with the rank of ensign. The prescribed uniform for the first day of DCA orientation training was called "Tropical Blue Long." I wasn't 100% sure I was even wearing the uniform correctly. There was one uniform item in particular that caused me to pause. It appeared out of place and felt inappropriate for me to wear, even though I knew it was authorized.

Pinned to my uniform, just above the left pocket were several Army ribbons. Seeing Army ribbons on a Coast Guard uniform looked a little out of place, but I was authorized to wear them. I had earned those medals and awards during my previous 7 years of service in the U.S. Army. There are significant stories, memories, and achievements associated with each one of those ribbons, so I was proud to wear them. However, the item pinned to my uniform just above the rows of Army ribbons looked out of place and felt awkward for me to be wearing: gold wings, gold Navy aviator wings.

Since December 1st, 1981, the date I graduated from Army Flight Training, silver Army aviator wings were proudly displayed on my uniform. However, on this day, my first day in a Coast Guard uniform, there were no silver wings. Instead, they had been replaced by gold Navy aviator wings. I felt a sense of disappointment, even betrayal, as I looked in the mirror at those gold wings pinned just above the rows of Army ribbons, where my hard-earned silver wings had once been.

I had spent the previous 7 years serving as an Army warrant officer and UH-1H helicopter pilot. I had earned the silver wings of an Army aviator by completing a year of rigorous flight training. After flight school, I served 2 years in South Korea, flying a multitude of demanding missions. I then served 4 years as an instructor pilot at Fort Rucker, AL, training new pilots who were all striving to earn their own set of silver Army aviator wings. Those wings were associated with memories of harrowing missions, many triumphs, gut wrenching tragedies, and the camaraderie of fellow aviators with whom I had shared the cockpit.

Direct Commission Aviator

In the Spring of 1987, I decided to apply for the Coast Guard's Direct Commission Aviator (DCA) program. I liked the idea of using my skills as a helo pilot to perform the missions of the Coast Guard, such as Search & Rescue, Environment Protection, and Drug Interdiction and more. The Coast Guard performs missions every day that directly impact people's lives. This was very appealing.

The Coast Guard sends some officers to the Navy for pilot training, but Navy flight school does not graduate a sufficient number of pilots annually to meet demand. To meet this shortfall, the Coast Guard gets a good percentage of its pilots from other services: Army, Marine Corp, Navy, and a few Air Force pilots. This is a great deal for the Coast Guard. They obtain experienced pilots whose training has been paid for by the Department of Defense. All the Coast Guard must do is train these already experienced pilots to fly a new aircraft and perform USCG missions, which is usually done in 6-8 weeks.

I exchanged, overnight, my hard-earned, slightly worn and weathered silver wings for the new shiny gold wings of a Coast Guard naval aviator. I wish I could have worn both my "old" silver and new gold wings, but by uniform regulation, this was not allowed.

So, as I stood there looking at those shiny new gold wings displayed on my uniform, I knew I had not earned them. I wondered how long it would take for me to feel like I had earned the privilege of being designated a naval aviator. For now, they were just a shiny adornment that felt out of place.

April 27th, 1996, on board the Coast Guard Cutter Hamilton, Bering Sea, Alaska

Nine Years Later – My First Deployment

I stood just inside the open hanger door, looking out over the helicopter landing deck. A vast expanse of ocean stretched out in every direction. No land in sight. It was a typical Bering Sea day.

Thick gray overcast clouds, which made the surface of the ocean appear dark blue, almost black. The visibility this morning was very good, probably 20 miles or more. Isolated rain showers could be seen here and there, dropping thick columns of heavy rain. Occasionally, a ray of sunlight would break through the overcast sky, briefly beaming a narrow beam of light down to the surface, like a spotlight, before slowly fading away. Sometimes, a ray of light would catch the edge of a rain shower briefly, displaying a rainbow, a rare treat in a world where shades of dark blue and gray dominated.

    The surface of the water was constantly in motion, rolling up and down, wave after wave. A few waves would curl and break at the top, then the wind would blow a puff of spray across the surface. White foam from the breaking waves was blown into elongated streaks across the surface. The flight deck slowly pitched up, the surface of the deck above the horizon far off in the distance, then dropped down again, the deck now below the horizon, before beginning another cycle upward. At the same time, the flight deck was pitching up and down, it was also rolling back and forth a few degrees to port and then back to starboard.

    The constant motion of the ship was the reason I was standing there, just inside the open door of the aircraft hangar, clear of the stiff, cold wind whipping by at about 40 knots. I stood looking aft, focusing on the horizon in the distance and breathing in the fresh air. I was *not* feeling well, but standing there was better than being inside the ship with its mixtures of smells and no visual references. I had been on board the ship long enough to know that the rolling motion of the ship doesn't make me feel seasick, but for some reason, the bow of the ship pitching up and then down as it plowed into the waves...well, *that* got to me. I don't know why, but it did.

    I was on my first deployment aboard a 378' Coast Guard Cutter, the CGC Hamilton. I had been in the Coast Guard nearly 8 years at that point but had never spent a night on a ship. I had been trained and qualified to perform ship landings and takeoffs, but I had never deployed as a member of an Aviation Detachment. My 1st duty station was Air Station Port Angeles, WA, but during my 4 years assigned there, deployments were rare, so I was never given the "opportunity" to deploy. (To be honest, I was not disappointed at the lack of opportunity.)

My second duty station was to Aviation Training Center (ATC) Mobile, AL, where I was a HH-65A instructor pilot. The mission of ATC Mobile is to train and evaluate pilots, not to deploy on ships. I spent a lot of time training and evaluating pilots on Coast Guard flight operations, such as hoisting to boats and deploying rescue swimmers, but ship operations was not one of them.

However, my third Coast Guard assignment gave me plenty of opportunity to make up for my lack of time at sea. I was now assigned to Air Station Kodiak, Alaska, as member of the ALPAT (Alaska Patrol). ALPAT's primary mission was to deploy HH-65 helicopters and crews aboard Coast Guard Cutters tasked with patrolling Alaskan waters, primarily in the Gulf of Alaska, the Bering Sea, and the Aleutian Islands. We deployed aboard the Cutters as their Aviation Detachment and members of the ship's crew for the duration of their patrol, which was typically 2 months long.

Irony

I stood at the edge of the hangar's open door, trying not to toss what little breakfast I had eaten that morning, and reflected on the irony of my situation. Nine years earlier, while still in the Army, I had thought, albeit briefly, about applying to the Navy to become a jet pilot. The movie *Top Gun* had just come out in theaters. I was an impressionable, gung-ho, 20-something young man, whose original desire was to fly airplanes. But the more I thought about it, the idea of being stuck on a Navy ship for months at a time in the middle of the ocean and away from family while having to land on a pitching, rolling deck at night and in bad weather did *not* sound very appealing. And to add to the irony, I had volunteered for this assignment to ALPAT and to be stationed in Kodiak, AK.

So, there I was, 1 month into a 2-month deployment, stuck on a tiny ship (compared to a Navy aircraft carrier), heaving up and down, rolling port to starboard with near freezing temperatures in the middle of the Bering Sea and with my wife and 2 kids alone on remote Kodiak Island, AK. I had volunteered for this…what was I thinking?!

The weather was forecasted to grow worse throughout the day and into the evening, so no flight operations were scheduled, which was disappointing. Flying provided a brief respite from the constant ship motion, broke up the mundane shipboard routine, and helped the days to pass quicker. But not that day. Instead, I wrote another letter home, read a book, and thought about watching a movie later in the wardroom—assuming I could get to feeling good enough to venture back into the bowels of the ship.

Medical Evacuation Mission

That afternoon, I was in my stateroom lying on my bunk reading the novel *Alaska* by James Michener. The ship was still moving as much as it had been earlier in the day, but I was feeling a little better. My phone rang, it was the ship's operations officer. He requested I come down to the Combat Information Center (CIC). There was a potential Search and Rescue (SAR) case developing. Before heading down to CIC, I called the hangar deck and advised the crew of the potentiality and to ensure the helo was ready for a launch. My copilot, Ron, was also in the hanger so I told him to meet me in CIC.

When I arrived in the CIC, several people were gathered around the chart table in the center of the room, including the ship's captain and operations officer. A fishing vessel about 100 miles to the northwest had a severely injured crewman onboard. Apparently, a large wave caused some equipment to shift, and the crewman had been caught between the shifting gear. He had several obviously broken ribs and possible severe internal injuries. The guy needed to get to a hospital ASAP. The fishing vessel had already turned toward us while our ship was heading directly toward them, thereby closing the distance as fast as possible. The plan was to launch the helo when the fishing vessel was about 70 miles away, rendezvous, hoist the injured man into the helo, and then bring him back to the Hamilton. The ship's corpsman would stabilize the injured man the best we could in the limited medical bay while the cutter turned southeast toward St. Paul Island. When our ship was within flying distance of St. Paul, we would launch again to transport the injured crewman to the airport at St. Paul where a Coast Guard C-130 from Air Station Kodiak would be waiting to fly him to Anchorage. It was a good plan.

It looked like we would arrive on scene with the fishing vessel around sunset, but it would be dark by the time we got back to the cutter. The weather was forecast to get worse as the night progressed, so there was some urgency to get going ASAP. If the sea state increased to the point where the ship exceeded maximum pitch and roll limits for helo operations, we could not safely takeoff or land.

We rolled the helo out the hangar, unfold the blades and finished the final preflight preparations. I then briefed the flight mechanic and the rescue swimmer on the mission. A litter was loaded aboard the helo since the fishing vessel did not have one that was certified for hoisting operations.

The cloud ceiling was at about 700 feet, and visibility was still 10 miles or more with isolated showers. We would need to fly around the rain showers to avoid any potential ice buildup on the aircraft, but this was doable, even in the dark, using the helo's onboard radar. By Bering Sea standards, this was actually nice weather. However, the winds and seas were still higher than I'd like, but I could deal with that.

The helo was cranked up and prepared for takeoff. The helicopter control officer (HCO) on the ship's bridge passed us "the numbers" over the radio, which consisted of the ship's current pitch, roll, list (in degrees), and wind information. The ship's pitch and roll were below daytime limits but right at night limits. Hopefully, we could complete the hoist and get back to the ship before it got any worse.

A Challenging Hoist

We arrived on scene with the fishing vessel about 30 minutes after taking off, just as planned, right about sunset. The vessel had a large open area free of rigging amidship, so this was determined to be our best hoist location. I briefed the crew on the hoist plan and then had Ron brief the fishing vessel's crew via the radio. We were ready. I moved in over the vessel and my flight mechanic (FM) dropped the weighted end of a "trail line" down to the 2 crewmembers waiting on deck, then I backed off, keeping the boat and hoist area in sight. The rescue swimmer (RS) attached himself directly to the hoist hook and the FM attached our end of the trail line to the hook. The crewmembers on the boat would use the trail line to pull the RS toward them as he went down, helping to minimize his swinging under the helo. My entire crew was very experienced. All of us had conducted many hoists in training and during live SAR operations. Everything was progressing routinely. So far.

Once on the deck, the RS unhooked from the hoist hook. The FM retrieved the bare hook, attached the empty litter, then hoisted it down to the fishing vessel. The RS unhooked the litter and we moved left and back away from the boat. The RS helped the injured man into the litter and got him strapped down and ready for possibly one of scariest rides of his life. A few minutes later, the RS gave us a "thumbs up" ready for pickup signal. The FM gave me commands to position us directly over the vessel's deck so the litter could be lifted straight up. The RS continued to hold onto the trail line still extending from the hoist hook down to the deck. This helped to prevent the litter from spinning wildly as we brought it up to the helo. Once the litter was clear of the deck I again moved back and left, keeping the fishing vessel in sight and maintaining our altitude. With the injured man now inside the aircraft, there was just one last item of "housekeeping" to perform: pick up the rescue swimmer. The FM sent the bare hook down one last time. With a thumbs up signal from the RS, I had the FM give me conning commands to position us directly over the deck for the pickup. We then moved in over the deck and plucked the RS straight up and back into the cabin. The FM disconnected the trail line from the hook and dropped it for the fishing vessel to retrieve and keep. Hoists completed, we departed the scene for the approximately 30-minute flight back to the ship. The hoisting operations went pretty much as planned. It was challenging but certainly not the most difficult hoist I'd ever done.

The mission had been a fairly routine operation so far with mildly challenging conditions. The rescue swimmer, also an emergency medical technician (EMT), checked our passenger's vitals and made him as comfortable as possible, but he was obviously in a lot of pain. We all relaxed a bit as we headed back to the cutter, the hardest and riskiest part of the mission now behind us. Or so we thought.

Worsening Weather and Darkness

There had been some twilight remaining when we finished the hoisting, but now, about halfway back to the ship, all hint of sunlight was gone. No stars, no twilight, and no lights on the surface. It was pitch black above, below, and all around. We were now flying totally on instruments about 500 feet above the water. I turned the controls over to Ron so he could get some stick time, and I radioed the *Hamilton* for an update on the weather at their location. The winds and sea state (waves) had picked up, and the visibility had dropped down to about half a mile. It was obvious we were going to have to execute an instrument approach to the ship. No problem, we practiced these types of approaches all the time.

There are two types of instrument approaches to the water, a manual approach and a computer approach. Since we had the ship on our radar, we could use the radar to get ourselves on to a final approach path. I thought a manual approach would be easier and quicker. Ron agreed. He would fly the approach down to water, just astern of the ship, with me backing him up. Once I had the ship and the surface of the water in sight, I'd take the flight controls and make the landing.

With our approach briefing and landing checks complete, I told the ship we were ready for "the numbers." The ship's pitch and roll motions were right at the limits for a night landing, with occasional rolls a couple of degrees past the limits. This was not going to be a fun landing, but we had no choice. We were in the middle of the Bering Sea, fuel levels dwindling, and with absolutely nowhere else to go except into the water. For a moment, I thought maybe I should not have asked for "the numbers." After all, ignorance is bliss, but at least now I'd know what to expect when I get over the deck.

I would need to "stick the landing," score a "10," and win a ship landing gold medal. In reality, however, an old piloting maxim applies: "Any landing you can walk away from is a good landing." I intended to strive for staying dry and walking away, hopefully, with nothing broken or on fire.

I used the helo's radar to guide us directly to the ship. The lights of the cutter appeared at about half a mile out, just as expected. As we crossed directly over the ship, I started the clock and we turned to our outbound heading. At 1 minute past the ship, Ron started a right turn to the final approach heading. Rolling level on the approach heading, Ron descended to 300 feet. In the previous 8 years, I had practiced or taught this type of approach 100s of times, but this was one of the few times I had to perform it in actual instrument conditions and with so much at stake.

At the appropriate time, Ron started our descent and slowed our speed. I had the ship on radar about 1 mile away, but I still couldn't see it. At about half a mile I started to pick up the lights of the ship. Ron continued to descend and decelerate; things were looking good. At about 200 yards astern of the ship and 50 feet above the water, I took over the flight controls and brought us into a stable hover. However, I was about to discover that my stable hover wasn't going to remain "stable" for long.

First Landing Attempt

On a 378-foot Coast Guard cutter, there is an obstacle that sticks up directly astern of the flight deck. This obstacle, the Close-in Weapons System (CIWS), sits higher than the level of the flight deck. Therefore, landing approaches to the deck are angled to the left or right, rather than straight in from the stern. The winds across the deck favored a starboard to port (right to left) approach, so I slid over to the right to line up with the approach line painted on the flight deck. Because I was in the right seat, as I slid to the right, I could no longer see the ship's wake, a very helpful visual reference for the surface of the water. Normally, this is not a problem, but that night was so dark that the ship appeared to be suspended in blackness. There was no horizon and the black water below melded with the blackness above. My landing light was on, but it was pointed straight down, and was not much help.

The waves continued to cause the ship to move up, down, left, and right. I then started overcontrolling the helicopter, following the motion of the ship up and down. The torque indicator (engine power indicator) started to fluctuate up and down as I moved the to follow the motion of the ship. I glanced at the radar altimeter in an attempt to stabilize the hover, but the visual illusion had messed with my eyes and my brain. My copilot was calling out the radar altimeter readings as they fluctuated from 25 to 75 feet. I realized I was getting vertigo due to the lack of visual reference with the horizon and the surface of the water. The motion of the ship was compounding the problem. I told Ron to take the controls and stabilize us in a hover, which he did. He could see the stern of the ship and the wake, giving him better visual references for maintaining a stable hover and not "chasing" the ship up and down as it pitched.

I explained to the crew that I had started to become disoriented and why. I asked Ron how he felt about doing the approach and landing from the left seat, something he was not accustomed to doing, especially at night and with this much ship motion. He said he'd give it a try and if he did not feel comfortable at any point, he would abort the landing and back off. I thought about telling him that no one would feel "comfortable" under those conditions, but I didn't want him to feel pressured to continue the landing no matter what.

I got on the radio and explained our situation to the helicopter control officer (HCO) who was located on the bridge of the ship. I knew the commanding officer (CO) would be right there, watching and listening. The HCO came on the radio and told us to take our time and let them know if we wanted the ship to change its course, speed, or lighting configuration. I replied with, "Roger, will do."

Our fuel indicator was steadily ticking downward, adding just one more thing to the stress of the situation. We really needed to get on deck within the next 10 minutes.

Second Landing Attempt

I radioed the HCO and again requested permission to land. The HCO cleared us to land and directed us to take our signals from the landing signal officer (LSO). The LSO was located on the flight deck right in front of the closed hangar door and provided hand signals to aid the pilots with the approach and landing. Ron started to move in. The deck was still moving…a lot! Ron crept in toward the landing deck doing a pretty good job of maintaining altitude and just letting the ship ride up and down without following the motion. However, every time the landing deck pitched down, Ron and the LSO would lose sight of each other until the deck pitched back up. Ron didn't want to hover any lower simply to try and keep the LSO in sight for fear the flight deck would rise up and smack us. After about 3 cycles of losing sight of the LSO, the LSO become concerned and gave us a "wave off" signal. A wave off signal is indicated by the LSO waving both arms over his head. Ron complied and began sliding right, which allowed him to see the LSO again and regain good visual reference with the ship.

Now the fuel was getting to the point of being critical. I knew we'd have one more shot at making the landing. The last thing I wanted to do was run out of fuel and be forced to ditch the helicopter in water. Ditching in the Bearing Sea, at night, in these sea conditions was "maybe" survivable for the helo crew since we were equipped and trained for such an emergency. However, we also had an injured passenger on board, still strapped into a litter. He most certainly would *not* survive.

Third Landing Attempt – Last Chance

It was time to change things up and try a different tactic. I got on the radio and talked with the HCO and CO. I needed them to the alter the ship's course to provide a wind from the starboard bow rather than the port bow as we had tried twice already. This change would allow me, in the right seat, to make an angled approach from port to starboard and hopefully give me better visibility of the ship and it's wake as I hovered. I also asked that they shine any spotlights they had onto the starboard surface of the water. Normally, when performing a night ship landing, the idea is to minimize bright lights, but I needed something to help me see the surface and give me more visual reference. The HCO agreed. They'd need a minute to make the course change and get the lights on.

The HCO then asked for our fuel state. I told Ron to advise the HCO we are at critical fuel levels and would definitely be landing one way or another on the next approach. I told Ron to also advise the HCO that a "wave off" was not an option this time. If the LSO became uncomfortable, he needed move off the flight deck to a safer location.

Ron, once again, requested permission to land and got the new wind, pitch, and roll numbers. Pitch and roll were still at the limits with an occasional roll over the limit, but the winds were now set up for a port to starboard approach. Then I did something I neglected to do on our previous 2 landing attempts. I prayed. It was merely a quick, silent prayer, similar what astronaut Alan Shepard, also a naval aviator, had prayed just prior to blasting off on a *Mercury* rocket to become the first American in space. I said, "Dear Lord, please don't let me mess up."

The approach to the deck went much better this time. The spotlights on the water helped provide a visual reference. The ship was still moving as much as during my first attempt, but I was able to maintain a more stable hover. The deck was still rolling and heaving up and down dramatically. I established a hover over the landing circle while maintaining sufficient altitude to prevent the deck from heaving up from below and smacking us. I was working hard to maintain position and watch the motion of the deck, trying to get a feel for the timing and magnitude of each pitch and roll. I was waiting for the right moment when the roll was nearing level and the pitch upward had reached its peak.

Stick It or Get Rolled Off

After watching several pitch and roll cycles, I saw the deck starting a roll from port to starboard as it was also pitching up toward me. This was it! I rapidly dropped the collective (the flight control in my left hand that moves the helo up/down) in one smooth continuous motion to full down, putting all the weight of the helo on the wheels. We would either stay put or get rolled over the edge of the flight deck as the ship continued its roll to starboard. I held my breath and waited as we rolled further and further to starboard, stopped, and began to roll back to port. I think the entire crew was stunned, relieved, and grateful not to be upside down in the ocean. As we started to roll back to port again, I keyed the microphone and yelled, "Tiedowns!", but Ron was already giving the hand signal to the LSO. The tiedown crew rushed in and strapped us to the deck. We could finally take a breath.

Four of the ship's crew came out to the helo, grabbed the litter, and took our passenger inside where he could be attended to by the corpsman. Since the ship was moving so much, I elected to just shut down the helo and chain it to the deck rather than trying to fold the blades and roll it into the hangar. We had to take off again in a few hours anyway. Our rescue mission was only half completed.

At this point, CGC Hamilton turned toward St. Paul Island. By 0800 the next morning, the ship would be within flying distance of St. Paul and it would be light again, so that was our planned takeoff time. A Coast Guard C-130 from Kodiak would be at the St. Paul airport waiting to pick up the injured fishmen and fly him to Anchorage. In the meantime, we would try to get a few hours of sleep, which I thought might be difficult given the adrenalin and stress of the last couple of hours. Surprisingly, I fell asleep almost instantly. I was exhausted.

The rest of the medical evacuation mission went off as planned. The weather was not any better by morning, but taking off from a ship and flying in the light of day was so much less stressful when compared to the previous night's events anyway. We meet the C-130 at the St. Paul airport, transferred our patient, and flew back to the ship. Mission complete. The next day we received word that the focus of our efforts, the injured fisherman, had undergone surgery in Anchorage and was going to be fine—thanks to everyone involved. It had truly been a team effort.

Green Gold Wings

Thinking back over my Coast Guard career, this mission stands out as the culmination of my transition from Army aviator to Coast Guard naval aviator. It was an 8½ year process, but I could now, with good conscience and pride, say I had earned my gold wings and accept the designation of naval aviator.

When the elements silver and gold are combined, it produces an alloy called electrum, which is also referred to as green gold. My Army skills, knowledge, and experience combined, over time, with my Coast Guard skills, knowledge, and experience produced something much more durable and meaningful to me than pure silver or pure gold.

My silver and gold wings had been combined and refined to become green gold wings.

Army Wings, Medals & Rank Insignia (left side), Coast Guard Wings, Medals & Rank Insignia (ride side) Photo: Guyant collection

The 378-foot Coast Guard Cutter *Hamilton*. Photo U.S. Coast Guard.

Chapter 7

"I Hope We Don't Explode"

As silver in a crucible and gold in a pan, so our lives are refined by God.
—Proverbs 17:3, MSG

July 12th, 1999, Coast Guard Group/Air Station Port Angeles, WA

Caught in the Maelstrom

I was on duty as the senior duty officer/aircraft commander taking advantage of the quite evenings to get some work done in my office. Even though my primary job at Air Station Port Angeles was to be a duty standing pilot, my secondary job, what is typically referred to as a "collateral duty" was to be the group support department head and group facilities manager. It was *not a* part time job but was in reality a full-time responsibility. In fact, the officers who were previously assigned to this position, none of whom were pilots, performed this job as their full-time assignment. This explains why I was still in my office, at 9 p.m. on a Sunday evening. I quite enjoyed the job but it did require a lot of extra time and effort...to do it well at any rate.

My phone rang, which at that time of night is usually a harbinger of some dire circumstance. It was the communications watch stander in the radio room. He said, "Commander, the GDO requests you come to the Operations Center. He's on the phone with a guy who's saying he and 7 others are trapped by a fire on Dungeness Spit." I told him I was on my way over. It was now time to switch hats and put on my primary duty hat/flight helmet.

My office was in the building next door, so it took me a minute to walk over to the Operation Center (OpCen). I wondered how someone could be trapped by a fire on Dungeness Spit. Dungeness Spit is a 7-mile-long narrow sandy strip of land extending into the Strait of Juan de Fuca. There are no trees, only grass and driftwood. I stepped out the front door of the Group Support building into a 30-knot (35 mph) tempest blowing cold and steady from the west. The wind had been light just a couple of hours ago, but winds in the Strait of Juan de Fuca can go from calm to 30 knots or more in a matter of minutes, catching people off guard, sometimes with deadly consequences.

As I walked over to the OpCen with the whipping wind at my back threatening to sweep my legs out from under me, memories of a tragedy that had struck the Port Angeles, WA, community 9 years earlier came flooding back to my mind. Back then, my dad and I came close to being caught up in the wind-driven disaster that had struck in the Strait of Juan de Fuca just north of Port Angeles that first weekend in May 1990.

Saturday, May 5th, 1990, started out beautiful and sunny with hardly a hint of wind. It was the first day of a salmon and halibut recreational fishing opening. More than 100 small fishing boats were out in the middle of the strait taking advantage of the beautiful day. My dad and I planned to go out and try our luck at halibut fishing. He had driven up from Olympia that morning and ran into a few traffic delays on Highway 101, so we decided to have lunch at home first.

Air Station Port Angeles had a very nice 22-foot Boston Whaler that could be rented to Coast Guard personnel. I had it reserved for Dad and myself to use that afternoon. The weather was beautiful as we drove out to the air station at the end of Ediz Hook, which is narrow sand spit extending into the Strait of Juan de Fuca. We went into the Operations Center to fill out the paperwork and leave a copy of our "float plan" with the duty officer. As I was completing the float plan, I happened to notice that the wind indicator was reading at 30 knots. I thought it odd. It had been nearly calm when we walked in only 10 minutes ago. I walked over to the window to take a look outside. Sure enough, white caps were whipping across the harbor! At that moment, I overheard a desperate voice yell, "Mayday!", over the radio, which was being monitored in the Communications Center by the watch stander. All hell had just broken loose in the strait!

The wind had gone from calm to 50 knots in the span of just 10 minutes, catching over 100 small boats far from shore. The seas built quickly to 6-8 feet in height. Within a few minutes, the radio was jammed with people calling for help. The ready helicopter was launched as well as a 41-foot utility boat. They did the best they could, finding and saving as many people as possible.

I came in the next morning to continue the search for missing boats and missing people. The bodies of 4 people had been recovered late Saturday afternoon, but a 5th person remained unaccounted. We searched along the western shore of Dungeness Spit where the wind had driven many of the boats and people caught out in the storm and unable to get off the water Saturday. The beach was littered with dozens of boats of all types and sizes. I was surprised more people had not died in that sudden windstorm. The body of the 5th person was finally located a few days later.

But now, 9 years later, that same peninsula of land jutting into the Strait of Juan de Fuca, that had been littered with the hulls of broken and abandoned boats, was apparently now on fire, somehow threating the lives of 8 people. I hoped this day would not end as tragically.

Trapped By Fire and Water

When I arrived in the OpCen, the GDO was just hanging up the phone after talking with the reporting source on Dungeness Spit. The GDO filled me in on the situation. There were 8 people staying overnight at the New Dungeness Lighthouse, which is located on the end of Dungeness Spit. Of the 8 people, 4 were children between the ages of 8 and 12. Two families had rented the Light Keepers House for a 1 week stay as "guest lightkeepers."

Earlier in the evening, someone had built a campfire on the beach several hundred yards to the west of the Dungeness Lighthouse. Whoever had built the fire apparently thought the fire was out or had carelessly walked away. The 30-knot winds blowing across the water from the west fanned the embers. The strong steady wind had acted as a bellows, igniting the driftwood and grass along the beach. Before long, all the dry driftwood and tall grass across the entire width of the narrow peninsula was on fire and being driven by high winds.

The fire was moving fast to the east, directly toward the Dungeness Lighthouse and the Light Keepers House. The occupants were trapped on the end of the spit, surround by water, and their only land bridge was cut off by a wall of fire burning toward them. It was high tide, so they could not go down to the beach and just bypass the fire along the water. The high tide also prevented any 4x4 vehicles from reaching them along the beach. The 30-knot winds made sending a shallow draft boat across the inside of the bay too dangerous. It appeared their only way out of this predicament was via helicopter. Well, they called the right people.

My copilot, Dave, was also in the OpCen, gathering information on the situation. Dave and I were both familiar with the helicopter landing pad on Dungeness Spit, which is located right next to the lighthouse. We could land on the pad easy enough and load up the passengers from there. We wouldn't be able to pick up all 8 people at once, so we would have to make 2 or maybe 3 trips to evacuate everybody. Our HH-65 helo just didn't have enough power or interior cabin space for that many people in one load. I told the GDO to activate the search and rescue alarm. The alarm would alert the hanger personnel to get the helo out of the hangar and ready to fly. Dave and I dashed upstairs to the locker room to change into our dry suits.

As I came back downstairs and began heading over to the hanger, the GDO stopped me. I told Dave to go on ahead to the hanger and get things ready. The GDO had just gotten off the phone with the people at the lighthouse. The fire was getting very close to the house, and they were concerned that burning ambers and heat might ignite the building. They were going to leave the Light Keepers House and move toward the eastern end of the spit to keep from getting surrounded by the fire.

Staying Ahead of the Flames

The situation was growing more urgent. The fire appeared to be moving faster than anyone had anticipated, forcing the families to move east to stay ahead of the flames. But moving east toward the tip of the spit also meant they would eventually have nowhere else to go except into the water. Their choices would be to endure the heat of the fire and potential burns or enter the cold water and face potential hypothermia.

I as I dashed out of the OpCen, I told the GDO to call the operations officer and tell him we needed to recall a second helicopter crew and get another helo airborne ASAP.

A few minutes later, Dave and I took off to the west into the howling 30-knot wind. As soon as we turned east, the glow of the fire some 15 miles away was easily visible though our night vision goggles (NVGs). Even without the NVGs, we could see the fire burning in the darkness of the surrounding water. The 30-knot tailwind give us an extra push to get us on scene fast.

I briefed Dave, the flight mechanic (FM) and rescue swimmer (RS) on the latest development. We would not be landing on the helo pad as previously discussed since the fire had spread that far already. Instead, we would locate on open area to land east of the lighthouse. I told the RS we would leave him on scene and take 3 kids and 1 adult in the first trip. We would fly them back to the Air Station in Port Angeles, then come back for him and the other 4 people. I knew fitting 6 people in back of the helo would be tight, but I'd cross that bridge when the time came.

With the strong tail wind pushing us, we arrived over Dungeness Spit in just a few minutes. I was surprised by the intensity of the fire. There are no trees on the spit, just piles of old driftwood logs and tall dry grass, but it was all burning in a line spanning the entire width of the narrow peninsula.

The fire had already swept past the lighthouse and Light Keepers House, which were now surrounded by flames. The buildings were not on fire yet, but I guessed it wouldn't be long before they also caught fire. The people on the ground had made a good call to leave the house. They would have been surrounded and trapped by the fire.

We spotted several flashlights shining at us through the smoke about 100 yards downwind from the front edge of the fire. We completed our landing checks and opened the door. The entire east end of Dungeness Spit was blanketed by smoke, but I could still see the ground. I picked a spot to land near the flashlights and made the approach. The area was flat but covered with tall grass, the same dry grass fueling the fire, so I knew we could *not* stay there very long.

As soon as we touched down, the RS unstrapped, hopped out and headed to the group of evacuees gathering about 100 feet off our nose. The group huddle around the RS while he quickly briefed them on our plan. I obviously could not hear their conversation, but I could see many arms gesturing, somewhat franticly, first pointing at us, then the fire behind them, then us again, then the fire again, then each other, but nobody was moving toward us. I called the RS on his handheld radio and told him we needed to get going. A few seconds later the RS ushered 4 people toward the helo, 2 adult women and 2 girls. No problem. They were all fairly small. I later found out that the men, 2 dads and 2 boys, had decided to have the ladies leave first.

With our 4 passengers now strapped in, I pulled power and performed a no hover takeoff to minimize kicking up sand and grass. The smoke was thick but we climbed through it a matter of seconds, leveled off at 500 feet and headed straight for the air station 15 miles away. I turned the controls over to Dave and radioed the OpCen with an update on our current position and number of passengers on board. The GDO advised us that a 2nd helicopter was getting ready and should be airborne shortly.

About 5 minutes out from landing, I saw the 2nd helo taxi out to the runway and takeoff. I called them on the radio to give them an update on the 5 people still on the ground and the status of the fire. I told them our landing spot had been fairly free of blowing sand and debris, but the fire might be too close to that spot by the time they got there. The operations officer, Ed, and his copilot, Mark, had hurried to the air station from home to get the 2nd aircraft airborne. They also had a flight mechanic and rescue swimmer on board. Ed doubted he could get the 4 remaining evacuees and our rescue swimmer in one load. They would be too heavy. He told us to drop our passengers off and head back to pick up any "stragglers" they left behind.

I took a moment to look behind me at our "survivors." The two moms had their arms wrapped around their daughters. They were all looking out the windows and seemed to be enjoying the adventure. One of the moms saw me looking back at them and said, "Thank you!" I couldn't hear her, of course, due to noise of the helo, but I could read her lips and see the gratitude in her eyes. I flashed her a quick "thumb up" and turned my attention to completing the before landing checks. Dave made the landing and taxied up to the hanger. As our 4 evacuees walked toward the hanger, I looked at Dave, keyed the microphone and said, "God, I love this job." He smiled and nodded in agreement.

Back for More

With our passengers now disembarked, Dave taxied us back out to the runway and we took off again. While Dave flew us back to Dungeness Spit, I called the 2nd aircraft to get an update on their position and status. Mark responded, stating they had landed and were picking up 4 passengers, the 2 men and the 2 boys. Their rescue swimmer was going to stay behind with our swimmer, and they would both ride back with us. Mark told me the fire had moved too close to our previous landing spot, so they had picked a position further to the east, not far from the eastern tip of the spit.

A minute later, the second helo radioed that they were airborne. We were still a few minutes from our second landing. I radioed the RSs still on ground and jokingly asked them if they wanted a ride back to the air station or if they'd prefer to swim back. Rescue swimmers are a special breed. They were superbly fit, swam like otters, excessively gung-ho, and a bit crazy in the head. Our RS responded with, "Sir, we talked it over and would prefer a ride *this* time, but if you don't get down here soon, this fire might force us to have to swim somewhere anyway."

I told him we were 5 minutes from being on deck. He then advised me that the that first spot we had landed on was now on fire and had moved further to the east. They cracked some chem light sticks so we could see their location, now about 100 feet from the beach at the eastern tip of the spit.

I took the controls back from Dave and made the landing. The distance between the front edge of the fire and the landing spot the swimmers had marked was a lot less than our first landing, but we didn't have much choice. We landed in a sandy, but level, spot free of driftwood obstructions. The FM waved the guys in toward the helo. They quickly strapped in and I pulled power to get the heck out of there.

The 30-knot wind was blowing lots of smoke mixed with some burning embers directly into our takeoff direction. I could feel the heat as I pulled power and climbed nearly vertical to get us above the smoke and embers as quick as possible. As we climbed out of that mess, smoke and embers briefly surrounded the aircraft, some of it drifting into the cabin through the open door. A thought went through my head as I saw the burning embers swirling outside the window: "I hope we don't explode!" This was a first for me. I had never before flown through fire, but I knew the chances of a stray ember causing us to catch fire, much less explode, was probably zero, but still, the thought did cross my mind.

We safely climbed clear of the smoke and headed toward the air station for our final landing. It was a very eerie sight. The entire end of Dungeness Spit was glowing red, still being fanned by the 30-knot winds. Fire surrounded the lighthouse and the other buildings, but they were still standing and did not appear to be on fire—not yet anyway.

Still Standing

The next morning, we flew back over the Dungeness Spit to assess the damage. It was easy to see where the fire had starting in the driftwood piles about 300 yards west of the lighthouse. Everything was burned black and brown to the east of that spot all the way to the water's edge on all sides of the narrow peninsula...except for one area. There was a large patch of green close-cut lawn surrounding both the New Dungeness Lighthouse and the Light Keeper House. Both of these building, and a few smaller sheds, were standing tall, gleaming white and totally unscathed.

Do not be afraid—I will save you.
I have called you by name—you are mine.
When you pass through deep waters, I will be with you;
your troubles will not overwhelm you.
When you pass through fire, you will not be burned;
the hard trials that come will not hurt you.
For I am the Lord your God,
the holy God of Israel, who saves you.
– Isaiah 43:1-3, GNT

Chapter 8

Final Landing

> *For everything there is a season, and a time for every purpose under heaven.*
> —Ecclesiastes 3:1, NIV

July 17th, 2000, San Juan Islands, WA

C.A.V.U.

It was a great day to be flying! Clear bright blue skies, sunshine, and no forest fire smoke obscuring the views. In fact, the visibility was so clear I could see Mount Rainer 120 miles to the south as well as the entire snowcapped Cascade Mountain range stretching all the way north to Mount Baker, which was now just a few miles to the east. In pilot lingo, this kind of weather was referred to as CAVU, meaning "ceiling and visibility unlimited."

I was on a SAR (Search and Rescue) mission in the San Juan Islands located at the northern end of Puget Sound. The San Juans are beautiful that time of year, covered with lush green forests and surrounded by stunning blue water. The channels and bays outlining the islands are dotted with 100s of sail boats, kayaks, jet skis, and pleasure craft of all types and sizes. If we were lucky, we might spot a pod of orca whales that inhabit these waters. There was practically no wind, so the water was smooth and sparkling in the sun.

Washington has a reputation for being overcast, foggy, rainy, and a bit dreary, which it can be during certain times of the year, typically the winter months. I have flown among the San Juan Islands during foul weather, weather quite the opposite from that day, and it can be quite challenging, especially at night. Throw in some strong winds, and it also gets very turbulent. But the weather in July and August makes up for the rest of year, and the natural beauty of Pacific Northwest is unbeatable.

As a Coast Guard helicopter pilot based in Port Angeles, WA, it doesn't get any better than what we had that day. I had been flying helos for over 20 years, and on days like this, I can't imagine doing anything else. However, my crew and I were not out on a sightseeing trip. We were working, but it sure was nice having such an amazing view out my "office" window.

A Probable Hoax

About an hour earlier, a Coast Guard telecommunications specialist standing radio watch in Port Angeles heard a radio transmission on channel 16, the maritime distress frequency. The person making the radio call said, "Mayday, mayday, we're on fire." That's all they said. No position. No description of their vessel. No number of people on board. Nothing else.

I was the senior duty officer for the day, so the communications watch stander called to brief me on what he'd heard. I told him I was on my way over to listen to the recording. I asked him to also contact the other pilot on duty with me and ask him to meet me in the Operations Center. The group duty officer (GDO) was already in the radio room.

We played back the recording of the radio call. "Mayday, mayday, we're on fire." The male voice was calm with no indications of distress in his tone. There were no other voices or sounds heard in the background. The transmission was received on just one antenna, an antenna perched on top of 2,400-foot-tall Mt. Constitution, on Orcas Island, in the San Juan Islands.

The GDO made a few phone calls to see if the transmission was heard by any other units or stations in the Puget Sound area. Coast Guard Group Seattle also heard the mayday call, but like us, only on the Mt. Constitution receiver. No other units heard the call. The San Juan Islands and the Mt. Constitution receiver are actually in Group Seattle's area of responsibility, so they become the SAR Mission Coordinator (SMC) and took the lead on this case.

The Seattle GDO and I talked on the phone. We both suspected it was a hoax radio call, but we couldn't know for sure, so we proceeded as if it were an authentic distress call. Group Seattle asked us to launch the ready helicopter and fly up to the San Juan Islands. I concurred.

Unfortunately, hoax radio calls happen frequently throughout the United States, but unless there is evidence to prove, or strongly indicated, it is a hoax, Coast Guard policy is to proceed as if it's authentic. Hoaxes costs tax payers millions of dollars annually, divert aircraft and boats away from real missions, and put responders at risk unnecessarily. If someone is caught perpetrating a hoax, huge fines and prison time are possible. However, it's difficult to catch hoax offenders.

There were still a couple hours of daylight remaining, and the weather was CAVU, so the mission risk was low. Group Seattle directed us to fly up to the San Juan Islands to search. I told the GDO to go ahead and hit the SAR alarm. He flipped a switch on the Command Center console, and a loud warbling klaxon alarm sounded throughout the base, alerting everyone on duty to prepare for a launch.

I dashed upstairs to the locker room and put on my dry suit. Even though it was July and the air temperature was 75 degrees, we still must wear dry suits year around in that part of the Northern Pacific region. Although the air was warm, the water was not. During the peak of Summer, the water temperature might rise into the low 50-degree range, which will cause a person to become hypothermic in a fairly short period of time. The dry suits are for the aircrew's protection, in case we should end up in the water.

I had a slight stomachache, which I attributed to just being hungry, so I grabbed a couple of granola bars and wolfed them down while heading over to the aircraft hangar. Dinner would have to wait until after the mission.

Tay, my copilot, was already at the aircraft and had finished the preflight inspection. As we were strapping on our survival vests, I gathered the crew around for a quick briefing on our mission. The crew on this mission consisted of a flight mechanic/hoist operator, a rescue swimmer/EMT, copilot, and myself. We strapped in, cranked up, and got airborne.

As soon as we were airborne, I instructed Tay to climb to 750 feet and head straight for Mt. Constitution, which was 40 miles away, but easy to spot on that beautiful day. I reminded the crew to keep a sharp eye out for airplanes. They were probably our biggest hazard. During the summer, lots of people fly to and from the San Juan Islands on float planes and other small aircraft. One of my biggest concerns was midair collision. I've had two *very* close calls in my flying career already, so my eyes were outside as much as possible, especially in this high traffic area.

Our search plan was to stay at 750 feet and circumnavigate the 3 biggest islands while looking for signs of distress, such as smoke, signal flares, signal mirrors, additional radio calls, and so forth. Seeing how it was such a nice day, with 100s of boats and other watercraft in the area, it was hard to believe a boat on fire would not have gotten someone's attention. The Coast Guard was also making radio calls over the Mt. Constitution transmitter, advising boaters of the distress call and to contact the USCG if they have any information.

We had been talking with Group Seattle throughout the flight, advising them of our position, areas searched, and the results. Of course, we found nothing thus far indicating a vessel on fire or other signs of distress. As we completed our search areas, I told Group Seattle that I suspected the call was a hoax and recommended that we suspend the search. A minute later, Group Seattle called back, clearing us to stand down from the search and return to Port Angeles.

By this time, the sun had set. We were north of Orcas Island, the northernmost island of the San Juans, so we climbed to 1,500 feet and turned to a heading direct to Port Angeles. This course gave us one last pass over the islands just as it was getting dark.

Throughout the flight, the "hunger pains" I had felt in my stomach prior to takeoff never subsided. In fact, they'd increased. I took the controls from Tay as we headed toward home, thinking that flying the aircraft would take my mind off the growing feeling of discomfort in my stomach. It was getting dark, and I could see the lights of Port Angeles across the water about 30 miles away.

With about 20 miles to go, I started to feel nauseous and began to sweat. During the flight, I had not said anything to the crew about my upset stomach because I didn't think it was a big deal. I asked Tay to take the controls and told him I was not feeling well. I then asked the flight mech and rescue swimmer, seated behind me, if they had any type of bag or container I could use, just in case I needed to vomit. I made it clear that this was not a drill or some kind of joke. I really was *not* feeling well. The flight mech handed me a plastic garbage bag. I swiveled my helmet microphone down away from my mouth...just in case. We were about 10 minutes from landing back at the air station and over the middle of the Strait of Juan de Fuca, so we couldn't just pull over and let me hop out.

In the 20+ years I had been flying, I have never gotten airsick, and I have flown in some of the worst turbulence and vertigo inducing weather you can imagine. I had never even gotten close to being airsick. I have been seasick a few times, but never had motion sickness in the air, so I knew this was not just "motion sickness." There was something seriously wrong, and I felt it was rapidly getting worse.

Lights Out

Looking out the front windscreen, I could see the lights of Port Angeles in the distance. Then my vision slowly began to narrow, with darkness moving in around the peripheries as if I was looking through a tube. I had never passed out before, but I knew this was a sign I was going to lose consciousness. As the tunnel grew narrower, I remembered something an old Army helo pilot had told me once many years ago. He was a Vietnam veteran who was full of tips and sage wisdom not taught in flight school. He told me once that while flying to "hot" landing zones in Vietnam they would lock their seat shoulder harnesses so if they got shot, they wouldn't slump over onto the controls, making it impossible for the other pilot to control the aircraft. As my vision grew narrower, I reached down with my right hand and pushed my seat harness lock lever forward, locking me in an upright position. That's the last thing I remember doing before everything faded to black.

When I become conscious again, my head was tipped back and I was looking up toward the overhead console. There was a face about 12 inches away, looking down at me, and I felt something pushing on the left side of my neck. The rescue swimmer, also an EMT, had come forward to the cockpit. He was looking at me, shaking my shoulder and saying over the intercom, "Commander, can you hear me?!" I quickly remembered where I was and that I had a bag in my hand, which was good, because as soon as I moved my head to look forward, I began to vomit, thankfully into the bag. Tay continued to fly us toward the air station. I could hear him on the radio talking to the GDO, declaring an emergency and requesting an ambulance meet us at the aircraft as soon as we landed. We were still about 10 minutes away from landing.

After few moments of some pretty serious vomiting, I felt better. I swung my microphone back up to my lips and was able to answer a few questions from the rescue swimmer. They were all *very* concerned. The RS said I was out cold for about 15 seconds. The swimmer was starting to check for a pulse on my neck when I "came back to life." Until I came to, they thought I had died! Well, I hadn't, obviously, but even so, they would still have a pretty unusual story to tell their kids and grandkids.

Tay landed us without further incident and an ambulance (another first for me) took me to the hospital. The ER folks checked me out, did a few tests, and kept me for observation. After a couple of hours, the doctor determined it was probably just food poisoning and sent me home. My wife came to the hospital and picked me up. At home, I continued to be sick on and off throughout the night.

My Last Flight?

One of the thoughts that went through my mind in those few minutes prior to landing was that this probably was going to be my last flight, *ever*. I had always heard that if, as a pilot, you pass out, anytime, anywhere, you'd never fly again. This was not how I wanted my flying career to end. I was only 38 years old and was not ready to stop flying.

The next morning, I had a follow up appointment with the Coast Guard flight surgeon at the air station. I was very dehydrated from being sick all night so he put in an IV. The CG doctor agreed that my sickness was probably due to something I ate prior to coming on duty the day before. He explained the reason I passed out was most likely due to a "vasovagal" physiological response. Because I had locked my shoulder harness, which kept me seated upright, I was not able to lower my head and the blood drained from my brain. The doctor said if I had leaned forward and put my head down, I probably would not have passed out. I made a mental note: "Unless being shot at, *do not* lock your shoulder harness."

I then asked the doctor the big question on my mind, "Am I going to be able to fly again, or am I permanently grounded?" He said he would have to submit a request for a medical waiver but would recommend I be placed back on flight status. Since my brief period of unconscious was explainable, I should be able to fly again in a couple of weeks.

I was shocked! I had already resigned myself to the idea that I was now grounded and I would never again pilot an aircraft. I felt enormous relief! My flight career of 20+ years was not over. The doctor left the room, and as I continued to lie there with an IV in my arm, I cried a few tears of relief.

After a couple of weeks, my medical waiver was approved by USCG headquarters. The Coast Guard was experiencing a pilot shortage at the time, so HQ may have been more lenient and open to granting waivers than if pilots were a dime a dozen. At any rate, I was cleared by the fight surgeon and put back on flight status.

Post-Traumatic Stress?

I was cleared to fly again, but something in my mindset had changed.

I was concerned it might happen again. What if it happened while I was flying single pilot? What if I was in the middle of a critical Search and Rescue (SAR) operation where lives were at stake? What if I was with a less capable copilot? What if...?

Every ache, pain, twinge, and rumble in my stomach had me wondering if I was okay to fly. Doubt and anxiety regarding my fitness to fly continued to grow over the next couple of months. I was beginning to look for reasons to cancel or shorten a flight. Short notice changes to the flight schedule or duty schedule impacted all the other pilots at the unit. I did not want to be "that guy," the unreliable one who needed a replacement for every little ache or sniffle. It was beginning to weigh on me.

Standing SAR duty became especially difficult. I'd lie in the bunk while on duty, praying we would not have to launch in the middle of the night. The "what if" question always lingered in the back of my mind. I was constantly evaluating my fitness to fly and stand duty. The doubts and questions were eating away at my confidence and desire to fly.

But I didn't tell anybody about what was on my mind, not even my wife. I prayed about it, resolved to just "suck it up," do my job, and try not to think about it.

But still, after several months of increasing anxiety and nagging doubt, I made the decision to hang up my wings and stop flying as soon as I could. I felt it was time for me to move on to a non-flying career. I had no idea what or where, but I did feel a sense of relief about my decision.

I submitted my request to retire from the Coast Guard as soon as I could be released. I resolved to gut it out and continue to fly missions and stand duty until my last day. When asked why I decided to retire, I'd say something about having met my goal of 20 years in the service and wanting to pursue another career opportunity. But I never told anyone the real reason why I decided to retire from the Coast Guard.

Last Flight

My last flight was on June 6th, 2001. It was just a routine patrol up in the San Juan Islands on a nice CAVU day, just like that fateful day last July which was prompted by a probable hoax radio call. I didn't tell anyone it was my last flight, even though I knew I would never fly as a pilot again. When we landed back at Air Station Port Angeles, there was no celebration or special recognition of the event like I'd seen happen for others. I did a routine post flight debrief with the crew like I'd done 1000s of times before, filled out the paper work, changed out of my dry suit and went to my office. I just quietly walked away from my final fight. I was embarrassed and disappointed with myself. I just wanted to put it all behind me and move on.

The only thing I did different to "commemorate" what would be my last entry in my flight log book was take my flight helmet and put it in my truck. I decided to keep it as a memento of the 6,220 hours I had flown over the past 21 years.

I should have talked to somebody about what I was experiencing those last several months. I kept it inside, which certainly made things worse. I thought post-traumatic stress (PTS) only applied to very serious traumatic incidents like crashes, loss of life, combat experiences, serious physical assault, and things like that. I had only passed out for 15 seconds then puked. That's all. It hardly seemed like it should be a PTS inducing incident. It was embarrassing. But obviously, it was traumatic in my mind.

I was embarrassed about my reaction to the incident and how it had affected me. I kept telling myself it should not be such a big deal, but I couldn't shake it. I prayed for God to take away the anxiety and doubt, but sometimes God answers, "No, there is a reason for this trial, this pruning. Trust Me." There was a reason, of course. I just didn't know it yet.

The End, but Not *the* Ending

While this was the end of my flying career, it turned out not to be the end of my Coast Guard career.

I had considered the possibility of an assignment to a nonflying position within the Coast Guard. But the positions opening up in the next assignment year did not appeal to me, mostly due to the locations. It would have required moving my family to a large city, like Oakland, CA, or Washington D.C. My kids were now teenagers, and if we did move, that would be where they most likely graduate from high school.

There was only one opening that had potential. The job was at the National Search and Rescue (SAR) School in Yorktown, Virginia. The position was a highly desired assignment and competition for it would be fierce. I figured it would be extremely unlikely that I could get such a high-profile position like that, so I proceeded with plan A and submitted my retirement letter.

Proverbs 16:9, NIV, says, *"In his heart a person plans his course, but the Lord determines their steps."* I believe God guides a person's steps in a variety of ways, such as closing some doors and opening others. He closed the door on my flying career just as He had opened it many years ago. But He was now opening the door to another path and many new blessings.

National Search and Rescue (SAR) School, Training Center Yorktown, VA

When the aviation assignments officer at Coast Guard HQ in Washington, D.C. received my retirement letter, he called me. He asked what it would take to change my decision to retire. The Coast Guard was short of pilots and he didn't want to lose another one. I simply told him I was "burned out" on flying and needed a career change. He asked me if there were any aviation staffed nonflying positions, I would consider. I told him there was only one: the National SAR School in Yorktown. It was a nonflying position but it had to be filled by an aviator. The job involved being the assistant chief of the National Search and Rescue School, the aviation subject matter expert, and a classroom instructor, teaching search and rescue planning and coordination. My extensive aviation and SAR experience would be very valuable in that position.

This was actually a "win/win" situation for the assignments officer and for me. He needed a pilot to fill this position, and I could continue to use my aviation and SAR expertise while remaining in the Coast Guard. This 4 years assignment would also provide me the opportunity to be considered for promotion to the rank of commander. I told him I'd need to talk to my wife and kids about it first. He gave me the weekend to think it over.

My wife was perfectly okay with another move, which I expected, but my teenage kids' reaction surprised me. They were actually excited about the prospect of moving across the country to Virginia and the close proximity to so many new places on the east coast, like Washington, D.C., and Williamsburg, VA. They saw it as the next new adventure. That settled it. I withdrew my retirement request and accepted the assignment.

The door to my piloting career had closed. The past year of "pruning" had been painful, but God was preparing me and my family for something better, for new growth. He opened a new door which led to many wonderful new friendships, adventures, growth opportunities, and of course, new challenges.

Pruning Is Violence!

Yes, the pruning blades remove the dead leaves and lifeless branches, but it also removes many branches that are new growth.

A properly pruned fruit tree is a mere skeleton of its former self. All the green is gone, the beauty is stripped, and it is just a few steps before being totally destroyed.

But oh, what amazing results!

Without the distraction of so many branches, the plant is able to poor all its life juices into the remaining ones. And the result? Larger, fuller, more beautiful fruit.

So, is the Word of God pruning me?
Yes.
Does it look violent at times and does it hurt?
Yes!
Do I hope to finally find value in bearing more beautiful fruit?
Definitely, yes!

—John Bartlett

Chapter 9

September 11th, 2001

> *Jesus answered, "I have said these things to you, that in **me** you may have peace. In the world you will have tribulation. But take heart; **I** have overcome the world."*
> —John 16:33, NIV

    I stood in the middle of the Yorktown Battlefield, the site where, in September and October of 1781, the final battle of the American Revolutionary War took place. The spot where I stood would have been directly between the British Army and the Colonial Army positions. It would have been very loud and very deadly, with canons and muskets firing across the field. But, at the moment of my visit, it was very quiet, eerily quiet.
    It was 5 p.m. on the afternoon of September 11th, 2001. I was on my way home from U.S. Coast Guard Training Center (TraCen)

Yorktown, where I worked at the National Search & Rescue School. The road to TraCen Yorktown passed directly though the Yorktown Battlefield, right past the location of the fiercest fighting during that famous battle, the battle that essentially ended the war and led to our independence from England. I had the privilege of driving through these hallowed grounds everyday as I drove to and from where I lived in Williamsburg, VA, to work at the TraCen.

It had been a surreal, confusing and emotional day for me, as it had been for nearly everyone in the world that day. I needed some time alone to reflect on the day's events before going home. I parked, walked up a small mound and stood looking over the battlefield. It was perfectly still, not a hint of wind blew. The sky above was perfectly clear and bright blue, not a single cloud or jet contrails in the sky anywhere. This is the East Coast, some of the busiest airspace in the country, so there were always jet contrails somewhere. But not on that afternoon.

That morning I saw and heard two F-15 fighters from Langley Air Force Base pass directly over the TraCen, heading north, flying low and very fast, their afterburners roaring. But now, there was nothing in the air as far as I could see. Actually, at that moment, there was nothing in the air anywhere in all of U.S. airspace, except for Air Force fighters.

A few sparrows and robins were flittering here and there, oblivious to the mandatory grounding of all flights nationwide. It was strangely quiet. Usually, an aircraft could be heard in the distance, operating from one of the many Army, Air Force, and Navy bases in this part of Virginia or from the busy International Airport just a few miles away. But at that moment, there was nothing but quiet, except for a few birds singing in the distance, grasshoppers flying from spot to spot, and deer munching on some dried grass about 50 feet away.

My great (x5) grandfather, Luke Guyant, had fought here, at Yorktown, over 220 years before, during the Battle of Yorktown. He was assigned to General George Washington's protection detail. As a 7th generation "Son of the American Revolution," and knowing that my great grandfather had been right there, it made that place on that date and that day's events even more surreal, more poignant.

As I stood there, I thought about the progression of my emotions throughout the day—from my initial skepticism of the news, then my confusion over reports of more planes crashing. As more news and video began streaming in on the TV, I felt disbelief. This couldn't really be happening! Then, as I watched live, the first tower fell and disappear in a cloud of dust. I was stunned. I stood watching speechless as were the others watching beside me. Then the second tower fell.

The 20 students in our Search and Rescue Planners Course had been in the classroom all morning and had no clue about what had happened. The school chief had all instructors and staff gather in the classroom while he interrupted training and briefed the students. Training was cancelled for the remainder of the morning so everyone could call their units, home, and/or loved ones.

Now, several hours later, as I stood in that serene setting, surrounded by the surreal silence, and imagined the ghostly presence of those who perished here to secure our freedom so long ago, I prayed. I asked God the same question millions of others were asking that day, "Why God? Why have You allowed this to happen to so many good and innocent people?"

Regardless of how deep and firm a person's faith in God, wondering how something of this magnitude fits into a loving God's omniscient existence and sovereign plan is a natural question. I already knew the answer to this question, but I still found it hard to fully grasp, understand, and accept, especially when directly impacted and so close to home.

When I got home, my 2 teenage kids, my wife, and I watched the evening news together. The reports, images, and videos were all about that day's barbaric attacks and the tragic aftermath. When the news finished, I turned off the TV so we could talk and share how we were feeling. I told the kids I was certain this day was going to have huge long-lasting impacts, not only on our country and the world, but potentially to each of us personally. At the time, I had no idea just how true that would be and how deep that impact would reach.

Sending Our Kids to War

Our son, Gordon, and our daughter, Jennifer, would both serve in Afghanistan. Our son deployed as a Marine Corp infantryman.

He was heavily engaged in fierce fighting in the Helmand Province of Southern Afghanistan. Our daughter deployed as an Army doctor and served at the NATO hospital in Kabul, Afghanistan.

My wife and I spent a lot of time on our knees praying for their safe return. I thank God for answering our prayers. Both of our kids did return home physically unharmed. However, there are wounds that are unseen. Those types of wounds take a lot longer to completely heal, if ever, and they may leave lifelong scars.

Got Questions?

Like many others, I have asked why bad things happen to good and innocent people.

The Bible, God's special revelation to us, does provided answers. There are also countless numbers of books, articles, and sermons that addressed this age-old question.

A resource I use frequently for biblical questions is **www.GotQuestions.org**. This source provides a good summary to an answer for this question. I've copied the response below. I pray you will find this helpful.

Why God?!

We live in a world of pain and suffering. There is no one who is not affected by the harsh realities of life, and the question "why do bad things happen to good people?" is one of the most difficult questions in all of theology. God is sovereign, so all that happens must have at least been allowed by Him, if not directly caused by Him. At the outset, we must acknowledge that human beings, who are not eternal, infinite, or omniscient, cannot expect to fully understand God's purposes and ways.

The book of Job deals with the issue of why God allows bad things to happen to good people. Job was a righteous man (Job 1:1), yet he suffered in ways that are almost beyond belief. God allowed Satan to do everything he wanted to Job except kill him, and Satan did his worst. What was Job's reaction? "Though he slay me, yet will I hope in him" (Job 13:15). "The LORD gave and the LORD has taken away; may the name of the LORD be praised" (Job 1:21). Job did not understand why God had allowed the things He did, but he knew God was good and therefore continued to trust in Him. Ultimately, that should be our reaction as well.

Why do bad things happen to good people? As hard as it is to acknowledge, we must remember that there are no "good" people, in the absolute sense of the word. All of us are tainted by and infected with sin (Ecclesiastes 7:20; Romans 3:23; 1 John 1:8). As Jesus said, "No one is good—except God alone" (Luke 18:19). All of us feel the effects of sin in one way or another. Sometimes it's our own personal sin; other times, it's the sins of others. We live in a fallen world, and we experience the effects of the fall. One of those effects is injustice and seemingly senseless suffering.

When wondering why God would allow bad things to happen to good people, it's also good to consider these four things about the bad things that happen:

1) Bad things may happen to good people in this world, *but this world is not the end.* Christians have an eternal perspective: "We do not lose heart. Though outwardly we are wasting away, yet inwardly we are being renewed day by day. For our light and momentary troubles are achieving for us an eternal glory that far outweighs them all. So, we fix our eyes not on what is seen, but on what is unseen, since what is seen is temporary, but what is unseen is eternal" (2 Corinthians 4:16–18). We will have a reward someday, and it will be glorious.

2) Bad things happen to good people, *but God uses those bad things for an ultimate, lasting good.* "We know that in all things God works for the good of those who love him, who have been called according to his purpose" (Romans 8:28). When Joseph, innocent of wrongdoing, finally came through his horrific sufferings, he was able to see God's good plan in it all (see Genesis 50:19–21).

3) Bad things happen to good people, *but those bad things equip believers for deeper ministry.* "Praise be to ... the Father of compassion and the God of all comfort, who comforts us in all our troubles, so that we can comfort those in any trouble with the comfort we ourselves receive from God. For just as we share abundantly in the sufferings of Christ, so also our comfort abounds through Christ" (2 Corinthians 1:3-5). Those with battle scars can better help those going through the battles.

4) Bad things happen to good people, *and the worst things happened to the best Person.* Jesus was the only truly Righteous One, yet He suffered more than we can imagine. We follow in His footsteps: "If you suffer for doing good and you endure it, this is commendable before God. To this you were called, because Christ suffered for you, leaving you an example, that you should follow in his steps. 'He committed no sin, and no deceit was found in his mouth.' When they hurled their insults at him, he did not retaliate; when he suffered, he made no threats. Instead, he entrusted himself to him who judges justly" (1 Peter 2:20-23). Jesus is no stranger to our pain.

Romans 5:8 declares, "But God demonstrates his own love for us in this: While we were still sinners, Christ died for us." Despite the sinful nature of the people of this world, God still loves us. Jesus loved us enough to die to take the penalty for our sins (Romans 6:23). If we receive Jesus Christ as Savior (John 3:16; Romans 10:9), we will be forgiven and promised an eternal home in heaven (Romans 8:1).

God allows things to happen for a reason. Whether or not we understand His reasons, we must remember that God is good, just, loving, and merciful (Psalm 135:3). Often, bad things happen to us that we simply cannot understand. Instead of doubting God's goodness, our reaction should be to trust Him. "Trust in the LORD with all your heart and lean not on your own understanding; in all your ways acknowledge Him, and He will make your paths straight" (Proverbs 3:5-6). We walk by faith, not by sight.

Why does God allow bad things to happen to good people?
Got Questions.org

Chapter 10

A New Calling

We are told to let our light shine, and if it does, we won't need to tell anybody it does. Lighthouses don't fire cannons to call attention to their shining—they just shine.
—Dwight L. Moody

In 2014, I started volunteering at a local elementary school. I was between jobs and looking for something productive to do with my time. My involvement in the school grew from a couple hours a week to a full-time daily commitment to helping teachers and their students.

Working with elementary school kids can be fun, frustrating, hilarious, disappointing, gratifying, disgusting, exciting, tedious, fulfilling, and exhausting—and this is all before lunch! Teachers experience all these emotions, and many more, all day long, every day.

So, what's it like to be a full-time elementary school volunteer and why do I keep coming back for more? Here's a snap shot.

December 6th, 2021, Horizons Elementary School, Lacey, WA

A Typical Morning

It was Monday morning, a little after 8 a.m. First grade students were trickling into the classroom. Most of the kids were happy to be there. They wanted to share their weekend adventures and traumas with anyone who would listen—a loose tooth, a scraped knee, the mischief their "Elf on the Shelf" created, a new kitty, a dog who puked in the car, a new "Dad Joke," a birthday party they attended, and numerous other highlights.

Most of the kids want to tell their stories to their teacher, but the teachers have limited time and can't get to everyone. So, I hang out, listen, react, and ask questions. The kids appreciate a minute of undivided attention from an adult, any adult who will listen to their stories. This is actually one of my favorite parts of each day.

On this particular morning, I was in the classroom listening to a boy tell me about a video game he played with his dad over the weekend. As I focused on the young lad, I happened to see the teacher, Mrs. Talley, moving quickly across the room toward a girl standing at her table where she had been eating a breakfast snack. The girl, Mary, had a hand over her mouth, and I heard her say in a slightly distressed voice, "I think I'm gonna throw up."

This is an event every teacher wants to prevent from happening in the classroom, at nearly any cost. Mrs. Talley started to usher Mary toward the classroom door. As she passed by me, Mrs. Talley told me she was going to walk the girl down to the school nurse, and then added, "Can you please watch the room?"

I said, "You stay here with your class. I'll walk her down." I took over escorting Mary to the nurse's office.

My mind kicked into emergency response mode, and I quickly develop a plan of action. I visualized the route from our present location to the nurse's office and then calculated the odds of making the entire transit before Mary tossed her breakfast onto the hallway floor. The odds were not good. So, in my mind, I visualized alternate stops along the way in case an emergency course deviation became necessary while in transit.

I determine the first divert location would be the sink in common area, just before we make a left turn down the hall. After we make the turn into the hall, there was a student's bathroom and sink on the left. That became the second emergency stop, if needed. Once we reached the double doors and turned left down the hallway, there was a water fountain on the left. Not a great option, but still better than heaving her breakfast all over the main hallway floor. Once we make the final left turn, it was a straight shot down the main hallway to the door of the nurse's office on the right. That was going to be the riskiest part of the transit. It was a long distance, about 50 feet, with no emergency bailout options along this hall. We'd just have to go for it and hope for the best.

We got past the coat cubbies outside Mrs. Talley's classroom when Mary brought her other hand to her mouth and made "that" sound, the one indicating vomitous eruption was imminent. I quickly steered her toward the sink. The first heave came one second too soon, nailing the floor in front of the sink, the doors under the sink, and front lip of the sink. Subsequent heaves hit the intended target, thankfully. I started yanking out wads of paper towels and handing them to Mary to clean her hands and face. I placed paper towels on the floor to indicated a "don't step here" zone. I was hoping no students walked in it, slipped, or tracked it back to the classrooms before the custodian could respond.

After a minute, Mary was feeling better, so I figured we could safely make the remaining trek to the nurse with minimal risk. I dropped off Mary with the nurse, gave her a quick briefing of the situation, and then headed to the main office, which is just a little further down the hall. I asked the ladies in the office to contact the custodian for a cleanup in the blue pod common area sink on the right.

I then headed back to the blue pod sink. Thankfully, it appeared no one had stepped in the contaminated area. I'm not sure how long it would take for the custodian to arrive, so I grabbed massive quantities of paper towels from the dispenser and started cleaning up the floor. I decided to leave the sink and cabinets for custodian—he has gloves, and I was certain he was used to this kind of operation. I stomached the floor clean up pretty well with no queasiness felt at all. I guess I was getting used to that sort of thing. The custodian arrived and took over, grateful that I had prevented tracking of the mess to other locations. I moved to the other sink and do a thorough inspection of my pants and shirt. Thankfully, I had been outside the "splatter zone," so there was no need for me to go home and change. I scrubbed my hands very thoroughly, applied numerous pumps of hand sanitizer all the way up to my elbows, and then headed back to class. It was 8:28 a.m. The day was off to a "great" start.

In the classroom Mrs. Talley was fully engaged in the morning's lessons. The kids were focused on her and listening...well, most of them were anyway. I quietly told Mrs. Talley that Mary was with the nurse and would probably be going home. She said, "Okay, thank you," and continued on with the lesson, unaware of what had transpired just outside her classroom. This was good. If I had not been there to step in and help, tremendous disruption and pandemonium would have ensued. It would *not* have been a good start to Mrs. Talley's day or week. I'm grateful I was there to take that burden off her already overloaded shoulders.

December 13th, 2021, Horizons Elementary School, Lacey, WA

Round Two

One week later, a little after 8 a.m., and during the typical Monday routine, kids were trickling in, hanging up jackets, unpacking their backpacks, talking with friends, filling their water bottle, and so forth. I was hanging out just outside the classroom, greeting students as they arrived, listening to stories, and encouraging them to keep moving and to get ready for class to begin. Then I noticed Adrian.

Adrian was a very shy little girl who doesn't talk much, but suddenly she was standing directly in front of me, eyes wide, and looking up at me like she really needed my attention. This was unusual for her. So, I knelt and asked how she was doing that morning. Without saying a word, she pointed at her mask covered mouth with both hands. I instinctively knew what she was communicating and what was about to happen. I thought, "I got this. I'm a seasoned first grade veteran. I know exactly what to do!" I stood up and quickly ushered her over to the closest sink about 10 feet away.

I was *not* prepared for what happened next.

Adrian leaned over the sink, pulled her covid mask down below her chin, and then...spits. I heard a single heavy wet "plop" in the bottom of the sink. That was not what I expected to hear. I looked down and saw a *huge* glob of congealed blood and mucus. Two thoughts instantly passed through my mind.

First, "What the heck is that!?" It was one of the grosses things I had ever seen. I fought the gag reflex instantly building in my throat. Secondly, I had seen enough science fiction movies in my life to know what was probably going to happen next. The "blob" was either going to start crawling out of the sink on its own or an alien was about pop out of poor Adrien's chest or mouth and then skitter across the floor.

So, as calmly as I could muster while still fighting the gag reflex, I told Adrien to put her mask back on and that I was going to walk her down the school nurse's office. I resisted the urge to scoop her up and run to the nurse, certain there was something seriously wrong. What I had just witnessed was *not* normal.

When we arrived at the nurse's office, I described to the nurse what had just happened, trying not to gag as I replayed the image in my mind. I was expecting the nurse's adrenaline to surge as mine had and jump into emergency response mode like I've seen in ERs on TV.

But no, she remained calm and simply asked Adrian if she had had a bloody nose last night or that morning. Adrian calmly gave a small nod and said, "Yes."

The nurse explained to Adrian and to me that blood from a nose bleed sometimes pooled in the sinuses when you sleep, congealed, then flowed out later into the back of the throat. Nurse Angie dismissed me, saying she'd return Adrian back to class in a few minutes.

As I was walking back to class, I patted myself on the back for not overreacting by picking Adrian up and running her to the nurse. I was also very thankful that I had not shared my "alien parasite" diagnosis with the nurse. Both reactions would have been embarrassing and maybe even gotten this "crazy man" banned from school.

Back in the blue pod common area, I figured I'd better go wash "the blob" down the drain before some kids found it and mayhem ensued.

With first graders, I frequently had the feeling that pandemonium was always lurking just under the surface, and it wouldn't take much for it to be unleashed: a spider on the ceiling, a fly buzzing around the room, a sudden snowstorm, flatulence, a substitute teacher, indoor recess, an unclaimed Pokémon card lying on the floor, and so forth. The "blob" in the wrong hands had the potential to instill utter chaos.

So, I rounded the corner and slowly approached the sink, mentally fortifying my mind and stomach for what I was about to see. I peeked into the sink basin and found...nothing. It was empty. The blob was gone!? I figured someone must have already washed it down the drain. I hoped anyway. Or maybe...it had crawled out on its own. I guess we'll never know for sure.

Lunch Time That Same Day

Three hours had passed since the "blob" incident. I saw Adrian sitting at her desk happily eating lunch. As I walked by her, she looked up at me with her beautiful brown eyes and gave me a shy little smile. I knew this was her way of saying thank you for the help I had provided her earlier that morning. My heart melted.

It's small moments like that which make my time and effort worthwhile and keep me going back. I also know that nothing, not even the threat of an alien infiltration into the school's ventilation system, would keep me away from helping these kids and their teachers.

But, I swear, if I ever see something unidentified "skitter" across the floor and go under the door to the custodian's closet, I am *not* opening that door unless I'm holding a flame thrower.

Each of you should use whatever gift you have received to serve others, as faithful stewards of God's grace in its various forms.
—1 Peter 4:10, NIV

A Waste of Time?

I started volunteering at elementary schools in 2014. I soon discovered that I liked the energy, activities, and "vibe" at the elementary school level. It didn't take long for me to notice that most teachers loved their students, loved teaching, and were highly dedicated to their profession, but they were also overwhelmed, stressed, and in some cases, burning out.

My primary focus as a volunteer has been on helping the teachers with whatever they needed. My desire has been to free up time they would normally spend on routine, mundane, and time-consuming tasks. I hoped my efforts would allow them more time to focus on lesson planning, teaching, and spending more time with their own families rather than taking schoolwork home in the evenings and working on weekends. Teachers do appreciate extra help, especially from consistent volunteers they can rely upon on a regular basis.

My involvement at school quickly grew because I saw the need and felt like I was making a difference in small ways, but still small things added up. I quit my part time job and become a full-time elementary school volunteer. The first couple of years I frequently asked myself, "What am I doing here? Am I wasting my time? Should I be doing something else more productive with my abilities, time, and experience?" I always came back to the same answer. This is exactly where I was supposed to be. You might say it was now my "calling."

A Deeper Motivation

Sometimes, I am asked why I volunteer at a public school where I have no family ties. Why am I not using my education, skills, and experience in more traditional endeavors, like most of my peers who have retired from the military and other people my age?

My safe or, maybe I should say, my "politically correct" answers to these questions are: As a way to serve and give back to my community, to be a positive male role model for kids, to play a small role in influencing the future leaders of our country, and to help overworked, unappreciated, and underpaid teachers with their awesome responsibility of educating future generations.

All of these answers are absolutely true and reasons enough to provide the motivation, encouragement, and fulfillment needed to keep me coming back. But, for me, there is a deeper, more foundational, motivation upon which the reasons I mentioned above reside.

> *In the same way, let your light shine before others, that they may see your good deeds and glorify your Father in heaven.*
> —Matthew 5:16, NIV

Volunteering my time, talents, and treasure at a public school is one way for me to put my faith into action. My desire is to be an ambassador for Jesus Christ and to be His hands and feet in this world. How is this done?

First, simply by serving others. By thinking less of myself and more of others and putting the needs of others above self. Secondly, by striving to live out what God's Word calls the "fruits of the spirit," which are love, joy, peace, patience, kindness, goodness, faithfulness, gentleness, and self-control.

But of course, I fail and fall short of these goals on a fairly regular basis. But that is where God's grace comes into the picture. It's not about working to earn God's favor, but rather it's about faith and God's grace. Period.

My time at school has greatly increased my appreciation for the very difficult job public school educators perform. Most teachers and staff I've known over the years are as dedicated to teaching and serving others as were the people I served with in the military. My "mission" for the foreseeable future is to support them anyway I can, which might mean, on occasion, dealing with potential school invaders, alien or otherwise, and other unusual situations.

Whatever you do, work heartily, as for the Lord and not for men, knowing that from the Lord you will receive the inheritance as your reward. You are serving the Lord Christ.
—Colossians 3:23-24, NIV

Chapter 11

It's Time

For the Son of Man came to <u>seek</u> and to save the <u>lost</u>.
—Luke 19:10, NIV

A very firm "thud" and the sound of rushing water left no doubt that we had hit the surface of the water. It was pitch black! I literally could not have seen my hand in front of my face, even if I had tried. But I kept a firm grip on the flight controls, afraid to let go and loose the only reference points I had. Though I could not see anything, I had a definite sensation of the aircraft quickly rolling over to the right. I was strapped into the right pilot seat, so that meant I would be going under water first. My training kicked in. I needed to hold on to my reference points, wait for the motion to stop, and *not* panic.

As the aircraft rolled over, I could feel the water starting to rush into the cockpit and envelope me. I planned to take one last fresh breath of air before my head went under the water, but before I could make that last gasp I was completely under water. I sat there holding the flight controls, waiting for the motion of the aircraft and rushing water to stop. The pressure on seat harness seemed to indicated I was now completely inverted.

After a few seconds the motion stopped. The next step was to reach to my right, pull the door jettison handle and push the door away, opening my escape route, all the while keeping my left hand on a reference point so wouldn't get lost inside the dark interior of a now submerged inverted aircraft. After jettisoning the door, I reached down with my right hand, released my seat belt and shoulder harnesses, and reached out with my right hand to grab the edge of the door to pull myself away from the aircraft. From there, it would just be a matter of swimming to the surface.

However, the door was blocked! Some obstruction was preventing me from egressing out my closest door. Remembering my training, I knew what to do. Keeping at least one handhold as a reference point, I had to pull myself over my seat and into the aircraft passenger cabin and then pull myself clear via the main cabin door. Just one small problem: there were 4 passengers in the back of the aircraft all attempting to find and exit through that same door, in total darkness, underwater, in an upside-down aircraft. And what about the copilot in the left seat? I had no idea where he was.

I continued to pull myself hand over hand until I felt the edge of the main cabin door. All I needed now was one strong pull and I'd be out and free to swim to the surface. But as I was about to pull myself though the door, a body slammed into me from my right, knocking me away from the door opening. No problem. I still had my handhold on the door's edge, so I just waited for a second for my turn through the door.

With the cabin door now clear, I pulled myself out the door and away from the aircraft. I suddenly felt something slam against my jaw, just under the edge of my helmet. Apparently, I was directly under the guy who had just exited, and as he was kicking his way to the surface, his steel-toed boot caught me in the face. The kick caused me to involuntarily exhale a puff of air and I felt a little dazed and disoriented, but thankfully, it didn't knock me out. I stopped swimming toward where I thought the surface was and just floated for a second trying to get my bearings.

I didn't feel panicked, not yet anyway. I just floated there suspended in the blackness for a moment. I knew someone was watching over both me and the others who had been in that aircraft with me. Sure enough, a second later I felt a hand grab my arm and push me upward toward the surface, away from the black abyss below and toward the light above, which I could not yet see, but knew was there.

I broke the surface, reached up to my face, and pulled the blacked-out swim goggles down, away from my eyes. I could now see the side of the large pool. The five other guys who had been in the aircraft simulator were already at the pool's edge. The Navy safety diver who had pushed me to the surface stayed alongside me as I swam to the edge of the pool. Once I grabbed the ladder to climb out, the safety diver informed one of the instructors that I had taken a pretty nasty kick to the side of my head and that I should get checked out by a medic.

Every 4 years, Coast Guard helicopter pilots are required to complete underwater egress training at one of the Navy's training facilities. On this day, I was at the 9D5 Underwater Egress Trainer, also simply known as "the dunker," located at the Naval Aviation Training Center in Pensacola, Florida. I had now completed 3 rides in the dunker and I needed one more to complete the required training. The last ride would again be with blacked out swim goggles, used to simulate a night crash landing in the water that required underwater egress from an inverted helicopter.

The Navy medic came over to where I was seated and checked me out. I wasn't bleeding, no teeth were missing, and my jaw wasn't broken. I told the medic I felt fine and was ready for my 4th and final ride. I wanted to get this over with and be qualified for another 4 years.

Nobody likes going through the dunker, but this training has saved the lives of many pilots over the years. This was my second time going through the dunker in Pensacola. My first dunker experience had been four years earlier when I was a new Coast Guard pilot learning to fly the HH-52 helicopter.

My 4th ride was completed without incident. With training now completed, I hopped in my van for the drive home. I now lived in Mobile, Alabama, where I was assigned to the Coast Guard Aviation Training Center as an HH-65 Dolphin instructor pilot.

As I was cruising down Interstate Highway 10, west bound toward Mobile, I passed by a highway roadside rest area. I remembered how, four years earlier, in October 1987, that same rest area was the location of a providential encounter which initiated a series of events culminating in a rescue, *my* ultimate rescue.

October 25th, 1987, Near Pensacola, FL

I was cruising down Interstate Highway 10, west bound in the Florida Panhandle and on my way to Mobile, AL, on a pleasant Sunday afternoon. The following morning would start four weeks of training at the U.S. Coast Guard's Aviation Training Center (ATC) in Mobile where I would be learning to fly a HH-52 helicopter. I had spent the previous 7 years as an Army helicopter pilot, but decided to get out of the Army and join the Coast Guard.

My wife, 6 months pregnant at that time, and our 2-year-old daughter were living with my parents in Olympia, WA, while I completed my training as a new Coast Guard officer and pilot. Upon completion of my training at ATC Mobile, I was to be assigned to Air Station Port Angeles, WA. Port Angeles was a small town in the far northwest corner of the United States on the northern border of Washington State, just across the Strait of Juan de Fuca from Victoria, British Columbia, Canada. I have never lived in nor even visited the Pacific Northwest, so I was looking forward to the adventure of a new job in a new location.

Coincidence is God's way of remaining anonymous.
—Albert Einstein

Providential Pit Stop

Up ahead, I saw a sign for a rest area 1 mile away, so I decided to make a pit stop. I passed by one car and then moved over to the right lane to exit into the rest area. There were plenty of open parking spots, but I needed to walk and stretch my legs, so I selected a spot at the far end of the parking area.

Before I could get out of my brand-new 1987 Dodge Caravan minivan, another car, an old Lincoln Continental, pulled into the parking spot right next to me. It was that last car I had passed on the highway just before exiting to this rest area. I was slightly perturbed that they decided to park their old, very worn monstrosity of a car right next to me. There were plenty of open, uncrowded, parking spaces available, but for some reason, they decided to park right there. I waited for them to finish pulling in and park before opening my door. As I got out of my van, careful not to let my door bang against their car door, I noticed that the driver and passenger of the other vehicle were an elderly man and woman. I smiled and give a friendly nod to them as I squeeze out my door and walked up to the sidewalk.

Bud and Reba

As I walked past the front of their car, heading toward the restrooms, I noticed a Washington State license plate on the couple's car. I wondered if they had just moved from Washington to retire in Florida and not had a chance to get their plates changed yet. I paused on the sidewalk not far from their car and waited for them both to get out. As they stepped up to sidewalk, I greeted them, pointed at their plates and said, "I see by your Washington plates that you're a long way from home. Do you still live in WA?"

The man replied, somewhat warily, "Yes, we do. We've been in the Tampa Bay area visiting family, but we're now heading back home." He was polite, but I could tell he was a little suspicious of this 20-something stranger singling them out for a conversation at a roadside rest area along an interstate highway in the far end of the parking area away from any other people.

I told them I was in the Coast Guard heading to Mobile, AL, for several weeks of training and then I was to be stationed in Washington. Once they realized I was in the military, they relaxed and opened up.

They told me their names were Bud and Reba. Bud said he was a retired Navy senior chief petty officer. They had several relatives who lived in Florida, including their daughter and some grandchildren, and they had driven cross country to visit them. They were now heading back to WA, via Los Angeles, where they intended to visit with more family first.

Reba pointed at my minivan and said, "That's a pretty large car for a single guy. Do you have a family?" I explained that my wife and daughter were already in WA, staying with my parents in Olympia while I finished my training in Mobile. I told them I hoped to be in Olympia by Thanksgiving Day.

Bud told me they had several Coast Guard friends in the town where they lived. Then he asked, "Where in Washington will you be stationed?"

"We're From Port Angeles!"

I told them I going to be assigned to Coast Guard Air Station Port Angeles. With that news, their eyes grew wide. They looked at each other, back at me, and with huge smiles on their faces exclaimed, "We're from Port Angeles! That's where we live!"

Bud and Reba had ended up in Port Angeles 20 years ago when Bud retired from the Navy. They spent the next 30 minutes answering my many questions and telling me how much we were going to love Port Angeles, the city, the natural beauty of the surrounding water and mountains, the great fishing, and the wonderful people.

Bud also mentioned a terrific church they attended with an outstanding pastor and lots of people our age with young children. He invited us to visit it when we got settled. I wasn't much of a "church goer," so I just nodded. They made Port Angeles sound like such an awesome place to live, and now I had already met two really nice people who lived there. Our visit was highly encouraging.

I only had about 60 more miles to drive to reach Mobile, but Bud and Reba still had over 3,500 miles to travel, so they were anxious to hit the road again. We said our goodbyes and wished each other safe travels. Bud handed me his business card with his home phone number written on the back and asked me to call them when we got settled in town. They wanted to meet my wife, daughter, and soon to be born baby. I stuck Bud's card in my wallet and promised I would, and then we departed ways.

That's too coincidental to be a coincidence.
—Yogi Berra

One Trillion to One Odds

As I continued my trip to Mobile, I could not stop thinking about our highly coincidental encounter. I thought about the odds of a chance meeting occurring in that fashion. Port Angeles has a population of roughly 15,000 people. How many of those people would be in Florida in mid-October and had driven the 3,000 miles to get there? Then what were the odds that they would be driving on Interstate Highway 10 in the same direction, at exactly the same time, pull into the same rest area, and of the numerous empty parking spots, happen to park right next to me? I have attempted to calculate the odds based on some conservative numbers, and the results are astronomical. Something in the area of one in one trillion. In other words, *extremely* improbable. Yet, it happened.

I could not help but think this was no accidental encounter. Something or someone had orchestrated this "chance" meeting. Who, how, and why, I had no idea. However it happened and for whatever the reason, it definitely caught my attention.

Mid-March, 1988, Port Angeles, WA

Bud's Business Card

We were now settled in Port Angeles. I had completed my training in Mobile, driven to Olympia, arriving the day after

Thanksgiving, picked up my wife and daughter, moved to Port Angeles in December, started my new job as a Coast Guard helo pilot, welcomed our son into the world in February, and bought our first house. The last 6 months had been extremely busy, with no small amount of stress associated with the many changes. But we were finally starting to settle into a routine. In Sun, my wife, was a real trooper. She was the mother of a toddler and an infant, living in a new house and a new unfamiliar location, with no friends or support from outside the home, and with a husband working in a new stress-filled career.

One morning, I was emptying a bunch of junk from my wallet. It was starting to get too bulky. I pulled out a bunch of old receipts, an expired Alabama fishing license, "punch cards" for Subway and Blockbuster, and so forth. As I was cleaning stuff out, I came across a business card, the card Bud had given me during our encounter in Florida nearly 6 months before. I wondered if Bud and Reba would remember me and our chance meeting near Pensacola, 3,000 miles away from Port Angeles. I showed In Sun the card with their phone number on the back. She remembered me telling her the story. I had called her the night I had arrived in Mobile and, while recounting my 2-day drive from Yorktown, VA, to Mobile, AL, had told her about the coincidental meeting of 2 people from Port Angeles. I decided to call and see if they remembered our chance meeting.

Reba answered the phone. I told her my name and that I was the Coast Guard pilot they met at the highway rest area in Florida last October. She exclaimed in excitement, "Of course we remember you! We talked about our meeting you all the way back home. Bud! Bud! Pick up the other phone! It's the young man we met in Florida!" Bud got on the phone and we spent about 30 minutes catching up on all that had happened in the last 6 months.

They had continued their trip home, via California, as planned and I filled them in on our major events of the last 6 months. Bud asked for the address of our house, which I provided. There was silence for about 2 seconds, then Reba exclaimed, "We're practically neighbors! We live just around the corner and down the street a bit!"

While we continued to talk, Bud again mentioned they attended a wonderful church in downtown Port Angeles and invited us to visit, if we had not already found a church to attend. We had not. In Sun and I had not really talked about attending a church.

After the call, I filled In Sun in on my conversation with Bud and Reba and mentioned their invitation to church. We decided that church might be a good way for In Sun to meet some new people in the area. Also, having our daughter attend Sunday School would probably be a good way for her make some new friends and provide an opportunity for her to play with other children her age.

Reacquainted

That next Sunday morning, we went to the Independent Bible Church, or IBC as the church members and locals called it. From the outside, it didn't look like a church. It was located downtown on one of the busiest streets in town. It had a stone and brick front, was narrow and 3 stories tall. There were businesses on both the left and right of the building. I eventually learned the building was originally built in 1915 as an Elks Lodge.

As we walked in the front door, the very first person I saw was Bud. He was an usher. We immediately recognized each other. I introduced him to my wife and kids. Then he "ushered" us into the church to see Reba, who was already seated. When she saw us, she jumped up and rushed over. She was *so* excited and many hugs ensued. It was like she was meeting her long-lost children and grandchildren.

Bud and Reba introduce us to many more people that morning, telling them the story of how we first met in Florida. Everybody was very friendly and welcoming. Port Angeles was a small town and the Coast Guard one of the major employers in the city, so nearly everybody knew someone who was currently on active duty or retired from the CG. We attended on Sunday morning once a month or so, and our circle of acquaintances slowly grew.

Wednesday Morning Breakfast

I read in the church bulletin that they hosted an early morning men's breakfast at a local restaurant each Wednesday. I had been invited several times by people at church but had never attended. A couple of months later, Bob, a fellow pilot I worked with, and I were talking about how my family was getting settled into the community. I mentioned we had attended IBC several times. Bob attended a different church, but he frequently joined the Wednesday breakfast before going to work and had, through that, gotten to know several men who attended IBC. He invited me to attend the breakfast with him, so I decided to check it out.

There were typically about 20 men at the breakfast from all walks of life: young and old, married, single and divorced, a couple of doctors, a county judge, an auto dealership owner, several retail business owners, a commercial fisherman, teachers, lumberjacks, and others. I enjoyed getting to know some of the men in this group, many of them longtime residents of Port Angeles. I viewed it as an opportunity to network and make some new contacts outside the Coast Guard.

I kept attending the breakfast whenever my work schedule allowed. I noticed most of the men brought a Bible into the restaurant with them. Not wanting to stand out, I found the one Bible we had at home, which had been giving to me when I was in eighth grade. I put it in my truck and brought it to breakfast when I attended.

A Men's "Retreat"

In March of 1989, the church, IBC, organized a weekend "get-a-way" event for any men interest in attending. The event would run from Friday evening to Sunday afternoon at Fort Worden State Park in Port Townsend, WA, with meals and overnight accommodations provided. Several men from the Wednesday breakfast, including Bob from work, were planning to attend, so I also decided to go. The overnight accommodations were in the old Army barracks on Fort Worden. Fort Worden and the old barracks were used as the setting for the movie, *An Officer and a Gentleman*.

On the Friday afternoon before the start of the weekend event, Bob had to change his plans, so he would not be going. I didn't really know anyone else who would be attending, so I also decided to back out. However, my wife insisted I go. She literally packed my bags and pushed me out the door. She knew it would be good for me. And she was right, as usual.

It was actually a pretty good time. We ate together, enjoyed some recreational activities: ping pong, playing cards, tossing frisbees and footballs around, basketball, walking the beach, and climbing around the World War II gun emplacements. It turned out to be a great time for getting to know other men in the community and building friendships.

In the evenings, we gathered together to sing and listen to a guest speaker speak about living as Christian men, as fathers, husbands and leaders. Forty men singing enthusiastically shook the rafters of that old Army chapel building. It reminded me of a few Friday nights at the Army Officers Club at Camp Humpreys, Korea, hanging out with the guys, everyone drinking and belting out bawdy Rugby songs and shanties, all led by some West Point Military Academy graduates. Except, on this Friday night, there was no alcohol, we were in an old Army Chapel and the songs were about Jesus. The sense of camaraderie was similar, but with a very different purpose and object of focus.

Pretender

Saturday night, after dinner, we all gathered once again in the old Army chapel. After more rousing singing, a guest speaker got up and shared another message. I don't remember the speaker's name or even the topic of his message. But it began to dawn on me that my "faith" was not real, was not authentic. I was faking it and pretending. If someone mentioned the Bible or church, I would say, "I'm a Christian too," but in reality, I was pretending to be a follower of Jesus the Christ.

I owned a Bible, but never read it. I attended church, but it was to "check the box" for my dose of religion for the week or the month. I went to the men's breakfast on Wednesdays, but it was mostly to network and build relationships. I had enough head knowledge to speak the lingo and use the right "buzz words" to fool others into thinking I was a believer and divert the conversation to another topic, but I was now beginning to realize I was just a "Christian" in name only. I was not really a follower of Jesus Christ, the Messiah...never had been.

It's Time

As I sat there in that old Army chapel, thinking about my epiphany and surrounded by over 40 men all listening intently to the speaker, I heard something. A small, quiet voice, not audible to my ears, but clear and unmistakable just the same. The impression, the small, quiet voice in my head, simply spoke two words, "It's time." That's all. But I knew exactly what those two words conveyed, and I knew exactly what I needed to do.

- It was time for me to stop being a pretender.

- It was time for me to stop thinking I was earning God's favor by checking the boxes I thought Christians were supposed check.

- It was time for me to stop being a "Christian" in name only, but to actually become a follower of Jesus, the Christ (the Messiah).

- It was time to admit I was a sinner in need of the Savior, unable to do anything to save myself.

- It was time to make a choice and accept the free gift Jesus offered me through His death, burial, and resurrection: the gift of eternal life with Him in heaven.

Just two simple words, "It's time." But I knew what they meant. So, I sat there quietly, closed my eyes, and had a sincere heart-felt conversation with God, probably my first ever. I admitted to God that I knew I was a far from a perfect person, a sinner, and I needed help to close the humanly insurmountable chasm between us. I admitted I knew there was nothing I could do on my own, except recognize I needed a redeemer and acknowledged that I needed the one who could reconcile my relationship with God. I needed Jesus.

I asked Jesus to be my Lord and Savior. In that instant, Jesus' sacrifice, His shed blood and death on that old rugged cross, bridged the insurmountable chasm and set me on a new path in this life on earth and the life here after.

When I arrived home the next day, Sunday afternoon, my wife knew as soon as she saw me that something significant had taken place. She told me she had been praying for me to see and understand where I stood before God and that I would see my need for the redemption provided for by Jesus' sacrifice on the cross. It changed our relationship and set our marriage on a new course.

Attention Grabber

Sometimes God's got to get our attention before we will listen. History is full of examples of the various ways God has done this. Saul, who would become the Apostle Paul, saw a bright light, heard a booming voice, and was blinded while on the road to Damascus, Moses saw a burning bush, the wisemen saw an unusual star and went to investigate, and Peter had a simple personal invitation to follow Christ.

Looking back, it's obvious that my encounter with Bud and Reba was *not* a coincidence. The 1 in 1,000,000,000,000 odds of having a "chance" encounter like that certainly got my attention. God used Bud and Reba to set in motion a series of events that resulted in the biggest life-changing moment of my life: that is, my decision to become a follower of Jesus. That decision changed me and the course of my life here on earth and life beyond this earth, for all eternity.

With the benefit of 20/20 hindsight, I see that God had placed others in my life prior to Bud and Reba. I either waved them off, ignored them, avoided them, or simply told them I already knew about Jesus simply to change the subject. But even so, they planted seeds.

What Bud and Reba did was very simple. They were friendly, willing to take time to engage in conversation with a stranger, showed interest in me and my family, and simply invited me to attend their church. That's all. God took it from there.

The Ultimate Search and Rescue

Jesus performed the ultimate Search and Rescue mission. He came to seek out sinners, which is *all* of us, and to save us from the consequences of our sin, which is eternal seperation from God.

That day in 1991, during underwater egress training when I was kicked in the face, I floated in the darkness, suspended between life and death. There was only one direction, up, that would lead to the life-giving air I needed. Any other direction led to death. If I had ignored or fought against the Navy diver who was there to rescue me, I would have drowned. Instead, I put my trust in him, and he guided me in the one direction to where I would find life.

While this is an imperfect analogy, it does provide a picture of what Jesus did for me, for all of us. The Navy diver that day didn't die saving me, but Jesus did. He died on a cross. If I had fought or resisted the diver's help, he would have forced me to the surface. Jesus doesn't force us. God has given us freewill to choose the saving grace provided by Jesus.

The choice is left to each individual person. I pray you will choose the Son.

Jesus answered, "I am the way and the truth and the life. No one comes to the Father except through me."

—John 14:6, NIV

God loves us and provided a way of reconciliation with Him. God's desire is that we recognize we are sinners in need of a redeemer. That redeemer is Jesus, God incarnate, who loved us enough to take our sins on Himself.

Is It Your Time?

God is trying to get your attention in some fashion. Of course, you have the option of ignoring, turning away, or even attacking God's attempts to share the good news He has for you.

The Lord is not slow in doing what he promised—the way some people understand slowness. But God is being patient with you. He does not want anyone to be lost, but he wants all people to change their hearts and lives. —2 Peter 3:9, NCV

Is God telling you that it's time?

- Time to examine God's Word for the first time or reexamine it?

- Time to stop trying to earn God's favor and acceptance?

- Time to stop being a Christian in name only?

- Time to talk with God, acknowledge you are lost and in need of rescue?

- Time to accept His free gift of salvation offered through Jesus?

For God so loved the world that he gave his one and only Son, that whoever believes in him shall not perish but have eternal life. For God did not send his Son into the world to condemn the world, but to save the world through him. Whoever believes in him is not condemned, but whoever does not believe stands condemned already because they have not believed in the name of God's one and only Son.
—John 3:16-18, NIV

Chapter 12

God Made a Farmer

Note: This chapter flashes back to my teen years. I thank God for the influence of my parents and my maternal and paternal grandparents. I believe the seeds for any success in my life, were passed down through multiple generations of farmers, and are rooted in the soil of central Wisconsin.

> *God said, I need somebody who, planting time and harvest season, will finish his forty-hour week by Tuesday noon, and then pain'n from tractor back, put in another seventy-two hours.*
> —Paul Harvey

Darcy D. Guyant

Zero Dark Thirty, August 1979, The Farm, Waupaca, WI

The Farm House

I laid there for a minute, listening. My bedroom was on the second floor of my grandparents' 100-year-old farmhouse. I could decipher from the creaks, squeaks, clangs, and other familiar noises what time it was, who was up, and what activities were taking place. I heard the familiar "creak" of the old wooden floor directly below me followed by the "squeak" of the front door opening. Those sounds acted as my wakeup call.

The "squeak" of the front door told me Grandpa had gone outside to get ready for the arrival of our first customer. From the kitchen, I heard pans clanging, the soft "thud" of the refrigerator door closing, and indistinct muffled voices emanating from the radio. Grandma was preparing breakfast.

My Farmer Heritage

It was the summer of 1979. I was living with my grandparents and working on their farm for the summer. At 17 years old, I was the oldest grandchild of Gordon and Arlene (Testin) Green. I was the descendant of a long line of farmers to reside in this part of Wisconsin, work this farm, and live in this house.

My great-great-great grandpa, Jacob Testin, and his wife Ellen, both immigrants from Ireland, married in 1857 and then settled in the central Wisconsin area, not far from where my grandparent's farm was located. Jacob Testin was a Civil War veteran, but not much is known about his involvement in the war. He died in 1895 at the age of 62, and his wife, Ellen, passed away in 1922. One of their 3 sons, Henry Testin married Caroline (McCauley), and they either purchased or homesteaded this farm in 1892.

My great grandpa, Harry Testin, was born in this house on December 15th, 1892. Then, 28 years later, in 1920, my grandmother, Arlene, was also born in this house, daughter to Harry and Iva (Wing). Another 20 years after that, my mother, Geraldine, was born to Arlene and Gordon Green, the first of five children. My mom was not born in this farm house but she did grow up here. I was now a 6th generation decedent of Jacob and Ellen Testin, and the 5th generation to live in this house and work on this farm. Even as a teenager, I appreciated the history of that old house and the rich farmland on which it sat.

Best Part of the Day

I threw back the sheets and rolled out of bed. It was 5:05 a.m. Sunrise was still 2 hours away. I got dressed quickly, headed down the very steep, creaky, and uneven stairs, slipped on my boots and jacket, and then headed out the door.

Pausing at the top of the steps, I took several deep breaths of the fresh, cool morning air. Any hint of sleepiness vanished. Stars filled the clear sky; there was no hint of sunrise yet. The air was perfectly still. I could hear cows mooing on a neighboring farm about a mile away, a cricket chirping in the grass next to the house, a whippoorwill calling in the woods across the road, and a rooster crowing somewhere far off in the distance. I heard a vehicle coming up the road, Testin Road, toward the farmhouse.

A minute later, a pickup truck pulled into the drive. Our first customer of the day had arrived. He backed his truck up next to the flatbed wagon, which was piled high with sweet corn we had picked the evening before. He loaded up on corn, probably 100 dozen ears, and other produce we had available (watermelons, potatoes, cantaloupe, tomatoes, squash, cucumbers, etc.), and then he headed to a farmers market at one of the small towns scattered throughout central Wisconsin. Grandpa sold his produce wholesale. Another customer was coming in about 30 minutes, so Grandpa and I worked quickly to get this first truck loaded up.

With our early morning customers loaded and on their way to the markets, Grandpa and I headed into the house for breakfast. We were met at the door with the smell of bacon, eggs, coffee, and cinnamon rolls. Breakfast is a big deal on the farm. We have a long day of hard work ahead of us, and we're going to need all the energy we can get. While eating breakfast, we listened to the local radio station: farm reports, weather forecast, yesterday's Milwaukee Brewers' ball game recap, as well as other local news and sports from around Waupaca County.

Sunrise

After breakfast, I headed back outside. The sun was just now peaking above the horizon. The first rays of sunlight caught the heavy dew on the leaves in field east of the barn. The dew shimmered like millions of diamonds sprinkled on the leaves. Brilliant rays of sunlight streamed upward from the edge of the horizon, catching distant clouds and creating streaks of yellow, orange, and purple high into the sky. It was a beautiful sight, but it only lasted a few minutes before fading as the sun climbed higher. It was cool at the moment, but the afternoon was going to be a scorcher.

Bees were already buzzing by, heading to and from Grandma's flower garden, which was near the horseshoe pit. I walked over to toss a few horseshoes while waiting for Grandpa. Grandpa was very good at horseshoes; he had trophies from past county fairs. I practiced when I could, but I never did beat him.

Grandpa came out a few minutes later and I joined him. We hooked up the now empty flatbed wagon to the tractor. It was time to go out and pick another load of sweet corn. Roger, my uncle, arrived as we finished hooking up the wagon. Roger helped us pick the corn, another 100 dozen or more, which he would then take to the Waupaca Farmer Market and sell on the Town Square.

Because of the heavy dew on the leaves, we were going to get soaking wet! The corn stalks towered over our heads, so we put on rain jackets and pants to help us stay a little drier.

Everything on Grandpa's farm was picked by hand, with the exception of potatoes. Grandpa had a "digger," which was pulled down the rows of potatoes by the tractor. A metal blade on the front edge of the machine dug into the dirt about 12 inches down, scooping the plants out of the ground. Then, via a series of conveyor belts, the machine shakes out the dirt, separates the plants, and conveys the potatoes up and into a large open potato truck, driven slowly alongside the digger. When the truck was full, the potatoes still had to be sorted, bagged, tied, and stacked by hand. I would sometimes count the number of 5, 10, 20, 50, and 100 pound sacks of potatoes I'd lift during the day. It wasn't unusual to heft over 4,000 pounds in an afternoon!

Grandma came out of the house with her big floppy sunhat on with a scarf tied under her chin to hold her hat on and climbed up on the tractor. Grandpa, Rodger, and I hopped onto the wagon for the ride out to the cornfield. At the field, Grandma lined the tractor up with some previously picked rows and slowly pulled the wagon along through the already picked corn stalks. The rest of us walked along beside the wagon picking the corn.

There is a technique to picking an ear of corn: firmly grasp the ear, yank down sharply while twisting with your wrist, snaping the ear off the stalk, then grab the next one and repeat. When your hands get full, usually about 6 ears, you toss them all up in the air toward the flat bed wagon, but not too hard or they'll fly over the other side. We each walked between two rows, grabbing, yanking, twisting and tossing. I usually got the rows closest to the wagon, so I didn't have to toss them as far. Grandpa and Roger took the rows further away. We could usually pick six rows wide as we slowly proceeded across the field. Grandma adjusted the speed of the tractor to keep the flat wagon abeam us. It didn't take long, maybe 45 minutes, to fill up the wagon to nearly overflowing.

Paul Harvey

After loading up Roger's truck for his trip to the farmers market, it was time for the morning coffee break. I changed out of my wet clothes first. The raingear helped, but it doesn't keep us completely dry. Then I headed down to the kitchen. Coffee break consists of leftovers from breakfast, pastries, toast, and homemade jam.

The distinctive voice of Paul Harvey saying, "Stand by for news!", came on the radio precisely at 9 a.m. To this day, whenever I hear a recording of Paul Harvey, I get a feeling of nostalgia as my mind goes back to those days on the farm and smells of Grandma's kitchen.

When Paul Harvey was finished, it was time to go back to work. The rest of the morning was filled with a variety of chores and harvesting activities: digging, sorting, and bagging potatoes, picking cantaloupe, squash, and a variety of other vegetables from the fields and garden, moving irrigation pipes, and hoeing weeds. On the farm, there was a never-ending list of tasks needing to be done.

After lunch, it was time to pick a wagon load of watermelons. Picking watermelons was probably my least favorite activity. They lay on the ground, and they were heavy! It was backbreaking work. Sometimes, you had to search for the melons among the tall thick weeds and the thistles. I hated thistles, the evilest of all weeds! They were tall, sometimes waist high, and very sharp. The thorns and spikey leaves are sharp enough to poke right through your jeans!

Weeds and Thistles

Six weeks earlier, Grandpa and I were in this same melon field hoeing weeds. The watermelon plants had sprouted and began to grow, but so had the weeds. This melon field was fairly large, about 300 yards long and 100 yards wide. You've probably heard the expression, "It's a long row to hoe." Well, I know exactly what that means, literally. At the time, it seemed like a waste of time. The weeds were small and the melons would grow large, so why bother, but I didn't question Grandpa. I put my head down and started walking between 2 rows, cutting off and digging up any weed plants. Grandpa had the two rows next to me. Up and back down the field we went for 3 hours, working our way from the south side of the field to the north.

Finally, it was time for lunch, but we had only finished half the field. I already had blisters on my hands, so I was not looking forward to coming back out in the afternoon heat to finish. However, after lunch, Grandpa had some higher priority tasks for us, so we never got back to weeding the other half of the field.

Six weeks later, we were back in the same field, this time to pick the melons. Looking across the field, it was very apparent where we had stopped weeding. The south half of the field had weeds but they were short and sparce. The melons were easy to spot and easy to pick. The other half of the field was a very different story. Weeds and thistles had grown tall, covering many of the melons. The weeds had choked out some of the sunlight and competed for water and nutrients in the soil, stunting the growth of many of the melons. The thick weeds and tall thistles also made our work harder, slower, and more painful.

Whenever I hear or read the "Parable of the Sower" in Matthew chapter 13 of the Bible, or the "Fruits of the Spirit" in Galatians chapter 5, I am reminded of that watermelon field.

It is certain that "weeds" will attempt to take root in our lives also. If we allow the unwanted, invasive, and useless plants to take root and grow unchecked, they can choke, entangle, and steal from our lives. Weeds will hinder the good fruit of our lives from maturing and possibly completely take over a life.

In order to thrive and produce the best possible fruit, we need to identify the invasive weeds of our life, cut them off, or dig them out by the roots before they get out of control and do real damage. We should continually ask ourselves, "What are the invasive weeds in my life that I need to do something about?" Identify them and then do something about them. It's sometimes hard work, but our lives will produce better fruit if we do.

Winding Down

After dinner, there were usually a few more chores to complete before winding down for the evening. Most evenings involved watching some TV: a Milwaukee Brewers baseball game, Lawrence Welk, Little House on the Prairie, the Waltons, and so forth. Before long, both Grandpa and Grandma would fall asleep in their easy chairs in front of the TV. I would slip out, take a shower, and then head upstairs to bed. There was no air conditioning in the old farmhouse, so my window was usually open, allowing the cool evening air to waft into the room. After a long hard day, sleep came quickly. I faded into a deep sleep with the sounds of crickets chirping outside, a whippoorwill calling in the woods across the road, and the steady "hum" of the yard light standing watch in the center of farm.

Grandpa's Legacy

My Grandpa worked 14-16 hours a day during the summer. I never heard him complain about the long hours or get upset when the weather didn't cooperate or grumble when a piece of machinery broke down. I never saw Grandpa get angry or even raise his voice. We didn't talk much while we worked, but when we did, it was usually about the weather, the crops, the Milwaukee Brewers, Green Bay Packers, or the Waupaca Lakemen (the local baseball team for which my uncle Roger played catcher).

Grandpa also grew up on a farm, not far from that one. His grandfather, Darius Green, moved to Waupaca County from Canada in 1856 at the age of 20. Darius Green initially worked as a farmhand, but then started purchasing property to begin his own farm, eventually growing it to 2,200 acres. Darius married Effie Garter in 1879 and they had 3 children. One of their sons, James Green, would marry Bertha Darrow in 1915.

James took over a portion of his father's property to farm as his own. James and Bertha had 8 children. Gordon, my grandfather, was the oldest.

Gordon met a girl, Arlene Testin, and they married 1939. In 1947 they took over Harry Testin's farm, the farm my grandma was born and raised on. Gordon and Arlene raised 5 children on this farm, one of which was my mom, Geraldine (Green) Guyant.

My son is named Gordon Wayne, the first names of my two grandfathers.

Unsung Heroes

Given my family's long history in agriculture, I'm sometimes surprised I didn't follow in the footsteps left by so many before me and become a farmer. When I was a kid, I thought being a famer would be a great life. You just plant some seeds, they sprout, rain waters the plants, the sun shines, and they grow all by themselves, producing fruits and vegetables. Then, after a time, you go out pick them and other people give you money for something the land produced for "free." What a great deal, or so I though as a kid.

In reality, farming is physically demanding and mentally stressful. There are many risks and uncontrollable variables: weather, pests, blights, mechanical breakdowns, fluctuating prices, interest rates, government regulations, competition, changing consumer demand, and so forth. But, if not for farmers willing to assume these risks, many of us would starve. Farmers are the unsung heroes of our country.

Please Google "Paul Harvey, So God Made a Farmer" and watch one of the videos.

During that summer in 1979, as a 17-year-old kid, I thought that maybe someday I could take over the farm when Grandpa and Grandma decided to retire. But God had other plans and opened other doors for me. My Uncle Roger purchased the farm from my grandparents in 1984 and raised his 3 daughters on the Green/Testin farm.

I did not become a farmer, but I am very proud of my family heritage. The time I spent working on my grandparent's farm was some of the most memorable and enjoyable of my youth. The life experiences and work ethic which took root in the fields of that family farm in central Wisconsin have served me well throughout my life. I thank God for that time and those memories.

That same day Jesus went out of the house and sat by the lake. Such large crowds gathered around him that he got into a boat and sat in it, while all the people stood on the shore. Then he told them many things in parables, saying: "A farmer went out to sow his seed. As he was scattering the seed, some fell along the path, and the birds came and ate it up. Some fell on rocky places, where it did not have much soil. It sprang up quickly, because the soil was shallow. But when the sun came up, the plants were scorched, and they withered because they had no root. Other seed fell among thorns, which grew up and choked the plants. Still other seed fell on good soil, where it produced a crop—a hundred, sixty or thirty times what was sown. Whoever has ears, let them hear.

—Matthew 13:1-9, NIV

The Testin/Green Farm
Photo courtesy of Rhonda Towne (Green) (my aunt)

Testin Family, left to right: Robert, Harry, Caroline (mother), Lea, Henry (father), Ellen, Ned.
Photo courtesy of Rhonda Towne (Green)

Henry and son Harry Testin
Photos courtesy of Rhonda Towne (Green)

Henry and son Harry Testin Harry and Iva Testin (approx. 1912)
Photos courtesy of Rhonda Towne (Green)

Five Generations, left to right: Geraldine Guyant, Arlene Green, Darcy Guyant, Jennifer Guyant, Harry Testin (1985).
Photo from the Guyant collection.

The next generation on The Farm, Gordon and Arlene Green with their 5 children: Geraldine (my mom), Roger, Rhonda, Richard, Genevieve. (1984)
Photo from the Guyant collection.

Gordon Guyant (my son) with his Great Grandparents, Gordon and Arlene Green. (1988)
Photo from the Guyant collection.

About the Author

Darcy Guyant was born and raised in central Wisconsin. During his senior year of high school, he discovered an interest in flying and earned a FAA Pilot Private Pilot license. Upon graduation from high school, Darcy was accepted into the U.S. Army's "High School to Flight School" program, graduating from Army helicopter flight training at Fort Rucker, Alabama, on December 1st, 1981, and was promoted to warrant officer, at the age of 19. Darcy flew the UH-1H "Huey" for six years, serving in the Republic of Korea and at Fort Rucker, AL, as an instructor pilot. While serving as an Army instructor pilot, he also attended Embry-Riddle Aeronautical University earning a Bachelor of Aeronautics degree.

In 1987, Darcy accepted a direct commission into the U.S. Coast Guard, beginning an 18-year career as a Coast Guard officer and helicopter pilot. Coast Guard duty assignments included Port Angeles, WA (twice), Aviation Training Center Mobile, AL, Kodiak, AL, and Training Center Yorktown, VA. His final Coast Guard assignment was as head of the National Search and Rescue School at U.S.C.G. Training Center Yorktown.

Darcy retired from the Coast Guard in 2005 at the rank of commander and with 25 years of military service. During his flying career, he logged over 6,250 hours of helicopter flight time, saving and assisting 100s of lives.

Darcy and his wife, In Sun, now live on a lovely lake near Olympia, WA. They have two children, Jennifer, an emergency medicine physician, and Gordon, a software engineer, and one precocious granddaughter, Gwenyth, who he loves to spoil. Darcy remains active in his church, particularly in children's ministry, and volunteers daily at a public school, assisting teachers and students.

One of Darcy's favorite activities is taking people out on their lake on his home-built wooden "raft" to enjoy the beauty of God's creation and maybe catch a fish or two.

CPSIA information can be obtained
at www.ICGtesting.com
Printed in the USA
LVHW020426281022
731594LV00009B/848